ALL ABOUT
ANGELS

ALL ABOUT

ANGELS

A. S. JOPPIE

 **Baker Books**

A Division of Baker Book House Co
Grand Rapids, Michigan 49516

© 1953 by Baker Book House Company

Reprinted 1995 by Baker Books
a division of Baker Book House Company
P.O. Box 6287, Grand Rapids, MI 49516-6287

Printed in the United States of America

ISBN 0-8010-5110-X

Introduction

Above us is another world, invisible to human sight, whose inhabitants are known only through the Word of God. Their range of knowledge is far above that of mankind. They have capabilities of managing great enterprises for God. They are a created order called "angels."

Angels held the flaming sword that guarded the tree of life in Eden. Angels took a family to safety from a doomed city and smote the wicked men of Sodom with blindness. They drove the chariots of fire through the sky and picked up one of God's prophets and took him to heaven. One angel breathed upon the military camp of the Assyrians and the earth was strewn with 185,000 dead. Angels walked into prisons and released apostles of the Church. As a ship was broken upon the reef, they stood with the apostle Paul assuring him of safety.

Angels are the appointed trumpeters to announce God's Judgment Day. They will open the seals of God's wrath upon this earth. An angel will stop the clock of time. The redeemed will enjoy their society in heaven. We shall walk with them amid the bowers, streams, and fountains of Paradise. We shall worship with them in God's great Temple. We shall soon join them to honor the King Eternal.

May **All About Angels** help you to know them better.

CONTENTS

1

Do Angels Climb Ladders or Fly?

I do not know why the great authors of the past and present have avoided writing on the subject of angelology, for the Bible speaks in a direct manner 248 times about these marvelous celestial creatures.

Some would have us believe that angels are weird, fantastic spirits of unfathomable mystery and unknown quality; but this is not so. The Bible tells us many interesting things about them: their creation, habits, character, activities, and service to God and man.

A Man and His Dream

Chapter 28 of Genesis gives us an interesting story. We look out upon a very lonely stretch of desert with nothing but barren waste and sand on every side. Rugged rocks are piled up here and there on the landscape. We see a solitary figure walking along a winding desert path. The man is young and full of vigor and strength, but the look on his face shows the lines of trouble, distress, and fear that haunt him. A hopeless, dejected air marks his countenance.

The day is growing late. The naked, haunting hills hide the setting sun. Darkness falls fast in the desert. Soon night enwraps the wasteland in a seamless mantle. No fellow traveler passes by. There is no inn by the way. The lone, weary traveler finds a place on the lee side of a rock for his night of rest. He places a stone for a pillow, spreads his robe about him, and from sheer exhaustion falls into a sleep like death.

To the weary wanderer, fast asleep in the noiseless desert, God gives a dream. A ladder reaches from earth to heaven. A number of angels are ascending and descending; the Lord of host stands at the top.

The Interpretation of the Dream

The Lord of hosts speaks to Jacob confirming the promise of a covenant made with his forefathers and assures Jacob of His personal interest in him. As Jacob awakens he takes a flask of oil and anoints the headstone of the night saying, "Surely the Lord is in this place" (Gen. 28:16).

But 1700 years of time were to elapse before Jesus gave us the meaning of this dream in John 1:51. It is very possible that Nathaniel had been reading and meditating on this wonderful story when Jesus spoke to him. How well the dream of Jacob reveals the mission of Jesus. As Jacob was a wanderer from home, so Jesus, the Son of God, was a wanderer from home. The foxes had their holes and the birds their nests, but the Son of Man had no place to lay His head. As Jacob was going forth to seek a bride from among his people, so Christ was going forth to seek a Bride—the Church. As Jacob was assured of God's presence and help, so Jesus was three times assured by the voice, "This is my beloved Son, in whom I am well pleased" (Matt. 3:17).

As the heavens were opened over Jacob, for his journey and task, so the heavens were opened for the Son of Man. The ladder that connected heaven and earth was a type of Jesus. The only way mankind can communicate with heaven is through Jesus Christ. The only way God communicates with mankind is through His Son, Jesus Christ. We shall see in another chapter that similar to the ascending and descending of the angels on the ladder, the earthly life of Jesus was a thrilling story of the ministry of angels.

10

A Look at the Nature of Angels

Their capital. Their capital is in heaven—the busiest place in the universe and the center of God's great empire—an empire of vast proportions beyond human comprehension.

Their intelligence. Their intelligence seems to be akin to that of God. Their knowledge of the secrets of the material and spiritual order of this world is far beyond the mental grasp of mankind. However, they do not seem to have the faculties to comprehend the complete plan of Redemption, for Peter said, "...which things the angels desire to look into" (I Peter 1:12).

This was typified by the angels in the Ark of the Covenant as they looked down upon the mercy seat. God has not revealed all His secrets to them, for they do not know the time of Christ's second advent. Jesus said, "But of that day and hour knoweth no man, no, not the angels of heaven, but my Father only" (Matt. 24:36).

The universe is their library. Each day they behold the rising and setting of a million suns like the one which enlightens our terrestrial globe.

Their number. Their census has never been taken by man; only God knows the exact number of this intelligent host. Saint John tells us that ten thousand times ten thousand minister about the throne of Jesus. This would be one hundred million. The Book of Revelation says there will be armies of angels who will come with Jesus in the great Day of the Lord. We do not know how heaven counts its armies. David counted twenty thousand rolling along the skyways in golden chariots, for he said, "The chariots of God are twenty thousand" (Psalm 68:17).

Ten thousands of angels came down on Mount Sinai when God gave the law to Moses (Deut. 33:2). The mountain shook and trembled while lightning flashed and thunder rolled, and Moses said, "I exceedingly fear and quake" (Heb. 12:21).

Do angels use their wings to fly? Isaiah (chap. 6) saw four of these wonderful creatures standing before the throne of God, each with six wings. With two he covered his face for reverence. With two he covered his feet for humble obedience. With two he did fly, for glorious service. They touch some great law of this universe with their wings. They are swifter than any typhoon. They are more radiant than any daybreak ever seen by man.

Their Commander-in-Chief. They are better organized than were the armies under General Marshall in World War II.

Their number is so vast that no man can comprehend the total. Their intelligence is akin to that of God. Their strength and power is so great that one angel can slay 185,000 soldiers in a night. They are creatures as deathless as God Himself. There are fleets of them! Squadrons of them! Millions of them! And they are all on the side of those who love and obey Jesus Christ.

It is glorious for the believer to realize that this vast host recognizes our Lord and Savior Jesus Christ as their Commander-in-Chief; for by Him and for Him were all things made in heaven and in earth.

2

A "Photograph" of an Angel

Would you like to see an angel? People travel across oceans and continents to see the beautiful scenes of nature. We enjoy gazing upon the wonders of man's accomplishments.

Variety and Beauty in Creation

The world about us abounds with variety in every realm. It can be said truly "variety beautifies creation." Scientists inform us that no two blades of grass are alike. Consider the trees of the forest with their numberless leaves, and not one leaf exactly duplicates another. We look at the countless stars in the heavens and we must say with the Bible "one star differeth from another in glory." The dignity of the Creator is glorified in this wonderful variety in creation. We also can expect things in heaven and the heavenly creation to substantiate this fact.

The beautiful array of colors in one flower garden reveals how the Creator's mind must enjoy the splendor of color. Consider the grandeur of the plant life in the depth of the sea, the beautiful colors in the aquatic organisms and the beasts of the field and jungle, and the gorgeous chromatic hues found in the birds of the air. Beauty, however, is made manifest in more things than just the array of color. There is majesty in the rocks that form the mountain ranges. There is glory in the richness and quiet of the valley. The endlessness of the

13

plains and the awesomeness of the desert show forth the matchless handiwork of the Creator. Contrast the small bubbling fountain and the silver streams of the rivers with the boundless seas, all made by the same God. Beauty everywhere reveals the glory of the Creator. Our God must revel in this endless variety in His creation.

We can naturally expect in the study of angels to find a variety in the angelic order and various ranks of power and authority. We also see an array of color and beauty among the angels that surpasses any known to mankind.

Everyone would like to see an angel, but it is very doubtful if you ever will see an angel until you get to heaven. If you can form a mental picture in your mind from a word description, we shall look at a "photograph" of one of God's great angels.

Michael, the Archangel for Israel's Defense

Michael is one of the great angels named in Daniel. "And at that time shall Michael stand up, the great prince which standeth for the children of thy people" (Dan. 12:1). This mighty angel is described in this passage as the angel that shall stand up—as a great prince—and defend the people of Israel.

"But I will shew thee that which is noted in the scripture of truth: and there is none that holdeth with me in these things, but Michael your prince" (Dan. 10:21).

This angel speaking to Daniel declares there is no other angel in heaven that stands with him in having the knowledge of these visions of future history. This angel also ascribes again the official title of heaven to Michael by saying "Michael your prince." "But lo, Michael, one of the chief princes, came to help me" (Dan. 10:13). Here the Scripture ascribes to him the title of Chief Prince. A correct Hebrew translation is *First Prince*. This portion of Scripture again presents Michael as the defending prince of Israel.

"...Michael the archangel, when contending with the devil, ...disputed about the body of Moses..." (Jude

1:9). Here again the heavenly prince Michael was meeting the devil, and demanding in the name of the Lord that Satan not molest the body of Moses. Moses was the earthly leader of Israel. He was their earthly captain and lawgiver. But Michael is Israel's heavenly defender.

Gabriel, the Messiah's Messenger

The second great angel named in Daniel is Gabriel. Several times Gabriel is named in this prophecy. We present our view that where Gabriel is not directly named, he is implied. Let us look at the Scripture

"And I heard a man's voice between the banks of the Ulai, which called, and said, Gabriel, make this man to understand the vision" (Dan. 8:16). The Scripture states that Daniel heard a heavenly voice. The voice identified the angel who was sent from heaven to give him the understanding of his vision as Gabriel. This is a positive declaration. The Messiah's messenger to Daniel in this vision was Gabriel.

"I am now come forth to give thee skill and understanding" (Dan. 9:22). Gabriel informed Daniel that he came forth from the Messiah to give him the spirit of revelation. He imparted to Daniel's mind the ability to understand his vision: "While I was speaking in prayer, even the man Gabriel, whom I had seen in the vision at the beginning..." (Dan 9:21).

Here again Daniel stated in a positive declaration that the angel whom he saw in the beginning of his vision was Gabriel. Daniel asserted that a heavenly voice identified this angel as Gabriel. Gabriel declared to Daniel that he was the angel sent from heaven to give him skill and understanding of the vision. In chapter 8:15-17 (Daniel) it is very clear that Daniel saw Gabriel in his glory. Daniel does not give us a description of the angel Gabriel until the angel speaks in chapter 10.

To suggest that chapter 10:5-6 describes some other creature or angel is to disrupt the entire book of Daniel. If Gabriel said that he was the angel sent from heaven to give him the understanding of the vision, why in the light of this truth do men insert a human being in the matter?

Gabriel has always been the messenger of the Messiah. Please note Luke 1:11:."And there appeared unto him the angel of the Lord standing on the right side of the altar of incense. And when Zacharias saw him, he was troubled." Three people on this earth have seen Gabriel. Daniel saw him. The father of John the Baptist saw him by the altar. Mary the mother of Jesus also saw him: "And the angel came in unto her, and said, Hail, thou art highly favoured, the Lord is with thee: blessed art thou among women" (Luke 1:28).

No man can deny that this Messiah messenger was Gabriel. "I am Gabriel, that stand in the presence of God" (Luke 1:19). Comparing these statements of Scripture with the passages in Daniel, we conclude that Daniel gives us in chapter 10:5-6 a wonderful and beautiful description of Gabriel.

The Sevenfold Description of Gabriel (Dan. 10:5-6).

1. He was "clothed in linen." Daniel had been praying and fasting twenty-one days when God sent Gabriel with the answer to his prayer. Daniel wrote in his prophecy a description of Gabriel; the angel was dressed in fine linen—what a robe! In all the descriptions of the angels found in the Bible giving any details of their appearance, they are clothed.

What is the meaning of linen? A fine linen robe was worn by the high priest when he entered the Holy of Holies each year. This robe had to be without spot or wrinkle when he went into the presence of God. This "fine linen robe" signifies access to God's presence. That Gabriel wore a robe like this suggests his access to God's holy presence at all times: "And the angel answering said unto him, I am Gabriel that stand in the presence of God" (Luke 1:19).

Saints will wear fine linen in heaven. Glorified saints who shall live in the presence of God forever are described in the Scriptures as wearing fine linen, clean and white. This signifies their access to God in heaven forever. The robes of the saints are described as made white through the blood of the Lamb, showing that mankind stands before God on the basis of the blood of the Son of God.

2. His *"loins were girded with fine gold."* What a girdle about the loins—fine gold! The gold signifies the likeness of Gabriel's nature to God—a nature sinless and pure! The fact that he is girded shows his readiness for divine service. Angels delight in the service of God. Also, the redeemed shall serve their God day and night.

3. His body shone *"like beryl."* Beryl is one of the most rare of all precious stones. Its color is hard to define; it is commonly described as green or greenish-blue. This color in the Bible stands for royalty. Remember that Gabriel is one of the heavenly "princes." Gabriel's image radiates the glory of his person, the light of his royal position and power in heaven—his entire body flashing, radiating the glorious light of greenish-blue! You will note that Daniel says that Gabriel shone "like the beryl" stone. This rich, gorgeous radiance of his royalty as a heavenly prince was beyond Daniel's description. What a day when we shall see Gabriel!

4. His face. The face is a map of the soul! It is a bulletin board of life. It tells what is going on in the heart and in the life. In this world we see hard faces and kind faces, pure faces and sensual faces, joyful faces and cynical faces. Nature has a way of writing its heart on the face! The face is the mirror of the soul! With deep interest we look into the face of the mighty prince of God, Gabriel.

Gabriel's face was like lightning, said Daniel. It must have been a dazzling brilliance. Daniel could think of nothing on earth with which to compare it. It was like the flashing of the lightning playing in the storm clouds!

17

With interest we notice that John says that the angel who rolled the stone away from the tomb of Jesus and sat upon it had a countenance like lightning. When the Roman soldiers, sent by Pilate to guard the tomb of the crucified Galilean, saw the face of this angel, they fell to the ground like dead men. Lightning—a dazzling terror to all evil doers. If the face of an angel reflects such astounding glory to sinners, small wonder, indeed, to think the world shall cry for rocks and mountains to hide them from the face of the Son of God. Some day this earth shall tremble. Men's voices shall call for strange things to take place, as they see the face of Jesus Christ (cf. Rev. 6:13-17).

5. *His eyes.* There are jealous eyes and greedy eyes. There are eyes that glow with hatred and eyes that gleam with love. What messages can be flashed to other people with just the eye. The wink of the eye has carried a message of deceit or, at other times, good will.

Gabriel's eyes were as "lamps of fire." This expression in Scripture signifies the seeing of "all things." The past and the present were an open book before Gabriel. In the message of prophecy that Gabriel brought to Daniel there were no "dark mysteries" to him. Gabriel's eyes were ablaze with the beautiful holiness which characterizes all holy creatures in heaven. They radiated holiness and power.

6. *His arms and feet were like "polished brass."* In the Bible, brass is related to judgment. This can be prophetic of the ministry of the angels. Angels, as we shall study in another chapter, will be the servants of God when He judges the earth. His angels will separate the sheep and the goats. The angels will winnow the chaff from the wheat. Angels will pour out the vials of God's wrath as described in Revelation. They will blow the trumpets and announce His judgments. Angels will go forth as the "reapers" who will gather all nations before Jesus

18

Christ for judgment. Angels will be the ministering servants of judgment. The arms and feet of Gabriel, glowing like burnished brass, signify his place in the judgment of sin.

7. *His words were "like the voice of a multitude."* There is something very marvelous about a voice. There are pleasant voices and harsh voices; there are charming voices and wicked voices. The "voice power" of angels is seldom mentioned. Paul says, "For the Lord himself shall descend from heaven with a shout, with the voice of the archangel...and the dead in Christ shall rise first" (I Thess. 4:16). The Bible makes it very clear there that the voice of Gabriel, the archangel, will play a very important part in the resurrection of the dead.

Daniel said that Gabriel's voice was like the voice of a multitude—a long, low rumble, powerful and forceful. Gabriel's voice must be akin to the voice of God! Gabriel has the high honor of standing in God's presence. He is the "prime minister" of God's kingdom. As heaven's prime minister he shall see that all the decrees of heaven's ruler, Jesus Christ, are fulfilled.

The "photograph" of an angel: His entire being pours forth a greenish-blue color like a beryl stone. His body is clothed in fine, pure linen. A girdle of fine gold is around his loins. His countenance is blazing like lightning, and his arms and feet are like burnished brass. His voice, with force and volume, is like the voice of a multitude. This describes Gabriel. It also reveals the glory and power of our Creator.

3

What Do Angels Do in Heaven?

The Bible, first and last, is a book that reveals God's plan of redemption. All other verities which it contains are second place to this cardinal truth. In the unfolding of this great redemptive plan, many other things are also revealed. Several inspired writers were given visions of heaven. Since heaven is the home of the angels, we would like to know what the angels do in this holy place.

All heaven at this time seems to be tuned to the redemptive plan of Christ. We know that God is from everlasting to everlasting. What the interests of God were before the creation of Adam and what the employment of the angels may have been is not revealed to us. When the plan of redemption is consummated and the kingdoms of this world become the kingdoms of our God and of His Christ, there no doubt will be a great change again even in the heavenly order of the angels. They are now sent forth to minister to the heirs of salvation. When Christ makes all things new the angels, like all the redeemed, will enjoy the day when Jesus Christ is acknowledged King of kings and Lord of lords. Our discussion in this chapter will deal with the present redemptive order.

Angelic Language
In I Corinthians 13:1, Paul declares that there is a

language of men and a language of angels. He states that if he could speak both in the language of men, and the language of angels but did not have love in his heart, it would profit him nothing. Are the language of the angels and the language of man the same? No one could contend for this point, for there are many languages now used by men on this earth.

The whole creation must have used one language in the beginning. God used a language when He spoke to Adam and Eve in the Garden (Gen. 3:9). Adam gave names to all the beasts and fowls (Gen. 2:20). Earth's new family—in Adam, Eve, Cain, and Abel—used this common language in communication. The serpent, Satan, used this language to induce Eve to rebel against her Creator. Eve then induced Adam through the medium of this language to transgress God's commandment.

Until man's sin and apostasy climaxed in the building of the tower of Babel, the human race spoke[1] one language. To check the swift advancement of sin, God punished mankind with a confusion of tongues. Many people deplore this language problem today. But the wisdom of God decreed this to check sin.

Because of the confusion of tongues at Babel—which was a curse of God—and of the complex development of languages, we must acknowledge it remains almost impossible to believe that any language of today could be the Adamic language.

But angels have a language. It has been revealed to us that they sing the praises of God in the holy courts above. They ascribe to God strength and glory (Ps. 29:1-2). They can shout for joy, for thus Job describes them in creation's morning. They hold council together in the heavenly courts (Ps. 89:7). The glory of the angelic tongue must be wonderful. It is the language of heaven. The redeemed in heaven will likely use the angelic language.

Angelic Singing

I have often been challenged with the statement that there is no passage of Scripture to support the belief that angels sing. Many agree that they praise God but that they never sing. We will state our viewpoint with the word of God: "When the morning stars sang together, and all the sons of God shouted for joy" (Job 38:7).

In this 38th chapter of Job, the Lord revealed to Job that when He laid the foundation of the earth, "the morning stars sang together." What a chorus this must have been. Their song rolled and swelled throughout God's vast domain. Following this grand chorus, "all the sons of God shouted for joy." A shout like this must have vibrated throughout all the heavens.

John describes the heavenly choir that ministers before the throne of God (Rev. 5:11-12). John says ten thousand times ten thousand angels stood before the throne. That would be one hundred million. What a host! But John adds to that number another figure—thousands of thousands. This is absolutely beyond human calculation. Verse 12 records the beautiful song of praise this numberless heavenly host sang to Christ:

> Worthy is the Lamb that was slain to receive power, and riches, and wisdom, and strength, and honour, and glory, and blessing (Rev. 5:12).

We know the angels are a higher order of creation than man: "Thou madest him a little lower than the angels" (Heb. 2:7). Since the angels are a higher order of creation, naturally their singing would be superior to man's in harmony and beauty.

All of God's children are looking forward to the day when they shall hear the angels sing. What gracious entertainment that will be for the redeemed—music and song without a minor refrain. Angels will be our neighbors some day.

22

4

Fourfold Nature of Angels

Angels Cannot Die (Luke 20:36)

"The Heavenly Host" of angels are a creation of God: "Praise ye him, all his angels: praise ye him, all his hosts...for he commanded, and they were created" (Ps. 148:2, 5).

The Holy Spirit often ascribes to God the title, "Lord of host." The "host" referred to are the holy angels. The Scriptures do not reveal exactly when this "host" was created; but we do know that they were created before this earthly globe on which we live came from the hand of God. Job declares that the angels shouted for joy when God created this world; therefore, they were a created order serving God before that time. Scripture further declares that man was made a little lower than the angels. So we learn that they were created before the human family began with the creation of Adam and Eve.

Angels are "ministering spirits." They do not have a body composed of the elements of which man's body is made; therefore, they do not grow physically. Time is not important to them. Their age is not determined by the method by which man reckons time. Being ageless they are deathless!

Of supreme interest in the study of angels are the many references made to them by the greatest authority on the subject of angels in the Bible—Jesus Christ, the master teacher Himself. Consider His words.

23

The Sadducees, who did not believe in the resurrection of the dead, asked Jesus this argumentative question. They declared they knew of a woman who had married seven brothers, the oldest first. He died, and likewise the other six. Therefore, if there was a resurrection and a life hereafter, which one of these brothers would have this woman for his wife?

The master teacher declared that redeemed and resurrected humanity would be like the angels, who "neither marry, nor are given in marriage" (Mark 12:25). The saints in eternity will be as the angels who are as deathless as God!

The author of the Hebrew epistle argues this point clearly against some teachers in the early Church who were contending that Jesus in His incarnation was not human but angelic: "For verily he took not on him the nature of angels; but he took on him the seed of Abraham" (Heb. 2:16).

If Jesus had been angelic He could never have died for the sin of the world. It was necessary for Him to take the form and nature of the seed of Abraham's race to be able to die. The form and nature of man enabled Christ to die for our sins upon the cross. As far as man's knowledge of God's wonderful creation is concerned, this world is the only part of that creation where there is death.

Only man dies. Taking the Scriptures as our guide, we find that man is the only creature with a soul who dies, which implies man with all his accountability to God. The creatures lower than man on this earth also die, but they are not rational beings accountable to God.

Man's death is the penalty of a broken law, and man finds life again only through the Lord Jesus Christ. "In Him is life." If men do not find Him, eternal death is their doom. Heaven is the home of the angels; it is free from the curse of sin and death. The holy angels

24

live in a realm of life. You will never find the grave
of an angel.

Angels Are Sexless (Matt. 22:30)

Our world of living creatures continues on the basis
of the laws of reproduction. Jesus declares the order
of the heavenly host is different. "They neither marry,
nor are given in marriage" (Matt. 22:30). We therefore
conclude that angels are sexless creatures.

Angels Are Holy (Mark 8:38)

The Bible speaks of "holy angels" in both the Old
and the New Testaments. All creatures who minister
in the courts of heaven are holy. A holy God reigns
in a holy heaven. Everything in heaven is free from
the contamination of sin. The vision of the youthful
Isaiah (Isa. 6) reveals that heaven resounds with, "Holy,
holy, holy, is the Lord of hosts: the whole earth is full
of his glory."

The blood of Christ will cleanse the sinner from all
sin and prepare him to associate with holy angels and
a holy God throughout eternity. A realm free from sin
is almost beyond human imagination.

But Angels Are Not Omniscient (Matt. 24:36)

Jesus implied that the acts and workings of God are
not known either to men or angels.

> But of that day and hour knoweth no man, no, not
> the angels of heaven, but my Father only (Matt.
> 24:36).

It is only as God is pleased to reveal His will that men
and angels understand. Whatever angels know, God
must reveal to them. Whatever man knows, God must
reveal to him.

All that this world knew about the first coming of
Jesus, God had revealed to man. All that angels and
men know about the second coming of Christ must be
revealed by God. Jesus did inform us of several things
that would indicate that His return was near. One outstanding revelation was that Israel would return to Pales-

tine. Our generation is now witnessing this great fulfillment of Christ's words. He declared the moral conditions of Sodom and Gomorrah would return. To the Christian's dismay and sorrow, these conditions are again on earth. Surely the angels understand and know these facts as well as the Church.

There is one glorious thing every sinner can know that angels will never know—and that is the knowledge and joy of sins forgiven.

What wonderful creatures the Bible reveals angels to be. It will be a part of our heritage in Christ to share with them the glory of the heavenly courts.

Angels Are Obedient

Angels obey their Creator. We do not know what moral code God has given them by which to live as a part of His wonderful creation. But they have received their moral responsibilities from God, and in a spirit of humble obedience they follow this code. There is not a disobedient angel in heaven! No angels run up the red flag in God's face saying, "No!" None stand in heaven's court and argue about orders. No one complains of his tasks or is envious of those of higher rank and honor. "Thy kingdom come, Thy will be done...as it is in heaven."

"As it is in heaven"—this is the ideal pattern. The heavenly kingdom provides all God's intelligent creation with a divine ideal. In God's kingdom obedience "is better than sacrifice and to hearken than the fat of rams."

Man in his fallen nature does not have the spirit of obedience. We, as sinners, are called "children of disobedience," and we are true to our name. Adam's race is ruined by the spirit of disobedience. The Second Adam (Christ) stands at the head of a new race—a spiritual race, truly called a "new creation in Christ." According to Hebrews 8:10-12, Christ writes the will of God upon the mind and heart of this new race, a people Scripturally classified as the people of God. This "born-again" race reflects and manifests the will to obey God.

"Lo, I am come to do thy will, O God!" This was the crowning spirit of our Lord Jesus. This is the manifestation of Christ in us. We delight in holy service. We glory in loyalty. Angels in heaven are examples of this loyalty to Christ. As members of His body, they respect, honor, and obey Christ—the Head.

Obedience develops faith. We have a wonderful statement of Abraham, the Father of the faithful: "Abraham obeyed." Obedience has the spirit of fearlessness in it. Peter said, "Shall we obey God or men?" Jails, prisons, and death itself were not shunned. Fiery furnaces and lions' dens were the scenes of heroic stands for God. Let angels and redeemed men forever stand as an army with banners, loyal and obedient to Christ, the Supreme Commander of the ages!

5

God's Royal Visitations

When one of a royal family makes a visit or a journey it is a matter of great importance because there are not many of these visits made. This earth is God's footstool, and though sin abounds and rears its ugly head to defy God's power and authority, God has not deserted this globe. There are eight royal visitations of God mentioned in the Scriptures.

Seven of these royal visitations are already matters of history, but the angels participated in some of these visitations. It will be interesting to notice that in the second and third visitations of God, angels are not mentioned. We believe there is a definite reason why they did not play any part in the royal pagentry on these two occasions. To follow God's movements, we shall take these eight royal visitations of God in the Scriptural order.

The Edenic visitation—"The Lord God walking in the garden" (Gen. 3:8). On this day of visitation God observed the entrance of sin and man's rebellion against Him. Man was hiding from God! This is the tragic reality of sin. The fearful and solemn questioning of God on this day surely foreshadows the great accounting day that is to come. What heart-searching questions: "Where art thou?" "Who told thee?" "What hast thou done?" When face to face with God man must tell the unvarnished truth.

There were no angels involved in this judgment. God directed the expulsion of man from Eden: "So he [God] drove out the man" (Gen. 3:24).

"He [God] placed at the east of the garden of Eden cherubims" (Gen. 3:24). Not only were these heavenly guards placed here to bar man's return to Eden but also a flaming sword was suspended over the gateway to Eden. These forever barred man from returning to his lost dominion. The human race started its eastward trend away from Eden. "And Cain went out from the presence of the Lord, and dwelt in the land of Nod, on the east of Eden" (Gen. 4:16).

The angelic sentinels and the flaming sword must have guarded Eden until the time of the Flood. Eden is never mentioned in Bible history after the Flood.

The Ante-diluvian visitation—"And the Lord shut him in" *(Gen. 7:26).* The Lord warned Noah that His spirit would no longer strive with man. Because God could no longer retard the awful corruption of man, He decreed the end of that race should come in one hundred and twenty years. This provided Noah with time to prepare the ark for the saving of his house. When the ark was completed and the allotted time had passed, God commanded Noah and his family to enter the ark. "The Lord shut him in." For forty days and nights the heavens above and the fountains beneath broke loose. Peter declares that the world that then was, was destroyed with water (II Peter 2:5; 3:5, 6).

Some people have doubted this story, but Jesus Christ our Lord reminded the people that this story was a part of the inspired record. Jesus said, "As it was in the days of Noah, so shall it be also in the days of the Son of man" (Luke 17:26).

There is no recorded visitation of angels during this judgment upon the earth.

The Babel visitation—"The Lord came down to see the city and the tower" (Gen. 11:5). This visitation of God in judgment has many things about it that are peculiar. In other judgments, God sent warnings to those to be judged through His prophets, or by angels, or by His own warning. Moses warned Egypt. Noah warned the world before the Flood. Jesus warned Jerusalem before it was destroyed by Titus in A.D. 70 (cf. Luke 21:20-24). The Church through her ministry today is warning the world of the final judgment of God. But the Babel judgment came unheralded. The reason why there was no forewarning of this judgment may be due to the fact that there was no death involved. The judgment accomplished two things.

First, the Lord scattered them over all the earth. What physical means God used to accomplish this fact, the Scriptures do not reveal. This was not a judgment that involved the loss of life. It was therefore a judgment of dispersion and not one of destruction, the only such judgment in all history.

Second, the Lord confounded their speech. Whatever the intent the builders of Babel had, Satan surely was perverting the plan and purpose of God. To check and thwart this plan of Satan, God confounded the use of a universal language.

The various languages of earth have been God's method of holding back the wide and swift spread of sin among the nations. There are no angels mentioned in God's ministry of judgment at this time.

The Sodom and Gomorrah visitation—"I will go down now and see" (Gen. 18:21). The words "Sodom and Gomorrah" speak volumes. When we wish to express sin and human degeneracy we say, "It is like Sodom and Gomorrah."

Abraham fell upon his face and prayed for this wicked dwelling place. The Scripture infers that the prayers of Abraham resulted in the escape of Lot's family from Sodom. Two angels went into the city of Sodom and smote a part of the evil men of the city with blindness. After bearing a measure of wicked insult, they succeeded in pulling Lot and his family out of Sodom. The next day Abraham looked toward Sodom, and it was as the smoke of a great furnace.

This judgment is often referred to throughout the Scriptures. The apostles of the Church used it as a warning. Jesus Christ referred to this demonstration of divine judgment. He also believed the story of Lot's wife, which is doubted by some. Jesus said, "Remember Lot's wife" (Luke 17:32).

The Horeb visitation—"God called to him out of the midst of the bush" (Exod. 3:4). In the solitude of the wilderness of Horeb a herdsman saw a strange sight. Fire was common in the hot, dry desert, but for a bush to burn and not be quickly consumed was strange, indeed! As the curious herdsman drew near, he was suddenly startled by a voice that called out from the bush. Twice his name was called. He was commanded to stand with unshod feet before the strange fire. Again out from the fire came these outstanding words, "I am the God of Abraham, the God of Isaac, the God of Jacob." He hid his face, for he was afraid to look upon God (Exod. 3:6). He heard another awesome announcement, "I am come down to deliver them [Israel]" (Exod. 3:8). The humble herdsman from Horeb went to Egypt. Plague after plague fell upon the land of the Pharaohs.

The fearful midnight hour was drawing nigh. The fathers in the household of Israel killed the lambs. With hysop they sprinkled the blood of the lamb upon the door posts. Midnight, dark and awesome struck. The angel of the Lord went throughout the land. The first-born of every creature lay dead in his wake. Israel fled. Egypt—despoiled, desolate, and impoverished—did not recuperate from the fearful judgment for many generations.

The Sinai visitation—"For the third day the Lord will come down" (Exod. 19:11). In Horeb and on Sinai, Moses met God face to face. No other earthly man has ever met God as Moses did. This royal visitation of God upon Mount Sinai is the most outstanding visitation so far studied.

In fact this visitation will not be surpassed until Jesus Christ returns in all His glory and stands again upon Mount Olivet—the glorious triumph of His second advent.

The Scriptures record some of the pageantry of this visitation. Fearful lightnings played about the crest of this mountain for forty days and nights. Awesome thunders rolled and echoed from mountaintop to valley. Winds whipped and sighed through the crevices and around the jagged rocks. Dark, black billowing clouds blanketed the mountain until the light of the sun could not be seen.

A royal announcer—the angelic trumpeter—preceded God to the mount. What fear and consternation must have swept through the encamped Israelites as the trumpet of God sounded. God was coming—and the angelic trumpter heralded His coming. The old mountain itself seemed to come to life, knowing its Creator was soon to set foot upon its crest. It staggered and trembled, its foundations groaned; the earth itself shook in fear.

As God came down upon Sinai, He was accompanied by twenty thousand angelic horsemen and royal charioteers! Horses of fire pulling chariots of fire, driven by angelic horsemen handling reins of fire! "The chariots are twenty thousands, even thousands of angels: the Lord is among them, as in Sinai" (Ps. 68:17).

In this psalm is the unanswerable Word of God. Twenty thousand chariots—twenty thousand angelic horsemen—accompanied God to Sinai.

David also says that thousands of thousands of other angels accompanied God to the mount. What a sight! The numberless host of heaven camping for forty days and nights upon Sinai. One lone man, Moses, stood amidst the awesome glory of these divine visitors. So "terrible was the sight" that Moses reported later, "I exceedingly fear and quake" (Heb. 12:18-21). No wonder the Scriptures report that Moses knew God face to face.

The Son of God's visitation—"Thou shalt call his name Jesus...He...shall be called the Son of the Highest" (Luke 1:31). Jesus said, after He began His ministry, "I am come down from heaven." The sinless life, the matchless message, and the love and light of His soul made an impact upon human history that can never be effaced. The life of Jesus from the cradle in Bethlehem's manger to its triumphant victory over death is a story of the angels. The angels hovered over His cradle. They rolled the stone away from His grave. They sat at the foot and head of the tomb. They first told the resurrection story. This wonderful life of Jesus is so revealing about the ministry of the angels that we have devoted an entire chapter to this study. For further information at this point study chapter ten.

Christ's next visitation. This eighth royal visitation is future. It is the next great event on the royal calendar of God. As the angelic horsemen were in the royal train of God as He descended to Sinai, so the white horse armies of heaven shall accompany our Lord when He comes again. As thousands of thousands of angels attended the divine visitor to Sinai, so Christ is coming in great power, and all His holy angels will be with Him. When great persons visit cities and nations, how the newsmen scramble to get their positions to take pictures. There is no need to further describe this royal visitation. The Holy Spirit, the author of the Word, gives us an advance "photo."

> And I saw heaven open, and behold a white horse; and he that sat upon him was called Faithful and True, and in righteousness he doth judge and make war. His eyes were as a flame of fire, and on his head were many crowns; and he had a name written, that no man knew, but he himself. . . . The armies which were in heaven followed him upon white horses, clothed in fine linen, white and clean.... And on his thigh a name written, KING OF KINGS AND LORD OF LORDS (Rev. 19:11-16).

The Lord announced to Moses that He would meet him the third day on Mount Sinai. The Lord has announced for this great future event the country, the city, and the exact mountain upon which the heavenly train will land.

And His feet shall stand in that day upon the mount of Olives [note exact mountain] which is before Jerusalem on the east [exact city named] (Zech. 14:4).

The country is none other than Palestine.

Jesus spent three years preaching in Palestine, and He usually walked. Once it is recorded that he rode, and that was to fulfill prophecy. He rode into Jerusalem upon the foal of an ass whereon no man ever sat. The ass is the symbol of peace. He rode into Jerusalem as the Prince of Peace. But the horse is a symbol of war. He shall ride a white horse when He returns to this earth in all His glory.

General MacArthur in his message to Congress said, "The whole epicenter of world affairs rotates back toward that area whence it started." This may prove to be one of the most sensational utterances of the twentieth century. God planted a garden eastward in Eden. This is the place where human history began. This also will be the place where human history will end. Joel 3:9-16 directs our attention to the fact that God will meet the nations again; the city and valley for the meeting place are already named. When God writes "It shall come to pass," it is not long before man writes, "It came to pass."

Are you ready for this royal visitation of God?

6

The Royal Chariot Drivers of Heaven

Horses and chariots in heaven! Angels in their immortal youth, unweakened by the ages, drive their beautiful chariots along the atmospheric highways of God. Does this seem too fantastic? Are you inclined to react with the statement that such things are irrelevant to the gospel of salvation, that they should be disregarded as insignificant and unworthy of serious consideration? Let God's Word settle your doubts and disbelief. First, we read in Psalm 68:17:

> The chariots of God are twenty thousand, even thousands of angels [Hebrew—armies of angels]: The Lord is among them, as in Sinai, in the holy place.

Earth's great warriors go down to dust; their swords rust with time; their banners fade and rot with age; but the royal chariot drivers of God live forever.

A Prophet Takes a Ride

A prophet riding in one of the heavenly chariots? Can you imagine such a sight? The Holy Spirit, the divine author of the Word of God, tells us of such event:

> Behold, there appeared a chariot of fire, and horses of fire, and parted them asunder, and Elijah went up by a whirlwind into heaven (II Kings 2:11).

Elisha, a fellow prophet, saw this wonderful translation and cried, "My father, my father, the chariots of Israel and the horsemen thereof." The Lord commanded one of heaven's chariot drivers to go down to earth to get Elijah and take him directly to heaven! Let us behold the heavenly chariot driver as he takes the reins of his steeds of fire, mounts his chariot, and descends for Elijah. With surprised adoration, Elisha watches while his master climbs aboard. He gazes with wide-open eyes upon the mysterious riders of the sky. Surrounded by all the celestial pomp that angels can afford, Elijah stands amidst the flaming squadrons of heaven.

As the heavenly train starts upward with the sound of a mighty whirlwind, God gives Elijah his physical change for the journey. He throws off his old prophet's mantle for the spotless robe of glory. Elisha picks up the mantle as a symbol of his answered prayer, "Let a double portion of your spirit fall on me!" Elijah went to heaven as no other man ever did as far as we know from Scripture. Elijah came back once since that day, when he appeared on the Mount of Transfiguration and talked with Jesus. His fellow traveler that day was Moses.

Elisha's Servant Sees the Chariots

Elisha had a servant who became very fearful one day. Elisha prayed that the Lord would cause his follower to see that there were more with him than there were on the side of his enemies. The servant's eyes were opened and "Behold, the mountain was full of horses and chariots of fire round about Elisha" (II Kings 6:17). Seen or unseen, they were there protecting Elisha that day.

Celestial Charioteers on Call

How thrilling to think of 20,000 royal chariot drivers of heaven with horses of fire, harnessed to chariots of fire! Angelic horsemen guide their flaming host of light and glory anywhere that God shall bid! God is not dead! The chariots are not unwheeled! God's wonderful army stands ready to defend all His interests on earth. The redeemed shall some day behold the royal chariot drivers of heaven. In a following chapter we shall study the armies of heaven.

7

Angels—Heaven's Militant Host

The superficial thinker might imagine that heaven is an ideal vacationland, a world where anyone can sit under his own beautiful shade tree and daydream his time away. Intelligent people, however, will recognize that a mighty empire as vast and wonderful as that of heaven must be a place of perfect organization, ruled by well-defined laws and principles. After a careful study of the subject we doubt if anyone will dispute that angels perform God's will in systematically arranged ranks of power and glory. Let us see how this vast host of creation is organized to carry out their duties in heaven. A later chapter will deal with their ministry on earth.

Michael—Commander-in-Chief

The name *Michael* in Hebrew means "who is like unto God." We must remember that God named His angels, and the bestowal of such a name is very significant. "But, lo, Michael, one of the chief princes, came to help me" (Dan. 10:13). *Chief* in Hebrew means "first." Therefore Michael is the first prince of heaven, and is here so recognized by the angel Gabriel as he talked with Daniel. His title is the highest of any angel; his rank in the heavenly order is first. This is seen in other portions of the Scriptures. "Yet Michael the archangel, when contending with the devil ... disputed about the body of Moses" (Jude 9).

The apostle Jude, under the inspiration of the Holy Spirit, declared Michael to be the archangel of heaven.

To our knowledge no other angel carries this honor and power. "And there was war in heaven: Michael and his angels fought against the dragon; and the dragon fought and his angels" (Rev. 12:7).

This verse presents Michael as the commander-in-chief of one of heaven's great armies. He is duly appointed by God to take his host and engage Satan in final combat, which will be the outstanding battle of the ages!

This will mark the beginning of a swift and final end for Satan and his organized hosts of evil. Thank God we have the advance news of the conflict. Michael and his host will be victorious. Heaven will be thrilled and hell will tremble when this news flashes through the heavens. Satan and sin will have made the headlines for the last time.

Gabriel—Heaven's "Telegram Bearer"

In Hebrew *Gabriel* means "mighty one." Entrusted with throne messages revealing God's plan in history, he is, indeed, heaven's mighty one. With messages which have come directly from the throne of God to the heart of man, he also is heaven's "telegram bearer."

It was Gabriel who brought to Zacharias and his wife the heavenly message that they would have a son who would be the forerunner of the Messiah. Truly, he was a great son—John the Baptist—the fearless wilderness reformer who was declared by Jesus to have been the greatest prophet ever born of woman.

Gabriel, heaven's "telegram" bearer, sought out a little Jewish maiden and told her she had found favor with God and that she would bring forth a son into this world, the long looked-for Redeemer.

What a "telegram!" What a Son who was born! Gabriel no doubt was behind the scenes directing the holy family down into Egypt and back again. It was Gabriel who was sent by God earlier to answer the prayer of Daniel, who, when a captive in Babylon, had prayed for twenty-one days. Gabriel gave Daniel gentile history hundreds of years in advance.

The angels "excel in strength" (Ps. 103:20). Because Gabriel played such an important part in the announcements of Christ's birth and prepared the way for His coming, I am inclined to believe that it was Gabriel who rolled the stone away from the tomb of Christ. This stone slab was eight feet in diameter and one foot thick, and it rolled into a groove in the rock to hold it in place. It weighed more than four tons. The women were troubled and wondered who would roll away the stone for them. When they arrived at the tomb, they discovered that an angel had rolled the stone away from the tomb and sat upon it. The angels are mighty in strength!

The Cherubims

The cherubims are first mentioned in the Bible in Genesis 3:24: "So he drove out the man; and he placed at the east of...Eden Cherubims, and a flaming sword which turned every way, to keep the way of the tree of life."

The cherubims are called in other places in Scripture, "living creatures." Their ministry in the garden of Eden and in heaven is defensive. It was their duty to guard the tree of life at the gates of Eden. We never read of the garden of Eden or the cherubims on earth in this respect after the Flood. As we look at the cherubims in heaven, we see that they stand on each side of the throne of God. "O shepherd of Israel...thou that dwellest between the cherubims, shine forth" (Ps. 80.1). "The Lord reigneth; let the people tremble: he sitteth between the cherubims; let the earth be moved" [Hebrew—Let the earth stagger] (Ps. 99:1). There are other passages of Scripture that describe these holy creatures as standing by the throne of God. Their ministry is a throne ministry. Therefore the Bible does not give us much information about them. We are dealing with matters pertaining to the throne of God. Christ is our High Priest at this throne. Some day the redeemed also shall stand before this throne. We shall know more about such wonderful created beings when we, too, stand in the presence of the King, and serve Him in holy delight forever and ever.

Seraphims

The seraphims are described by Isaiah: "I saw...the Lord sitting upon a throne, high and lifted up, and his train filled the temple. Above it stood the seraphims: each one had six wings; with twain he covered his face, and with twain he covered his feet, and with twain he did fly. And one cried unto another, and said, Holy, holy, holy, is the Lord of hosts: the whole earth is full of His glory" (Isa. 6:1-3).

Seraph comes from the Hebrew root, which means "love." Truly God is love. Isaiah does not inform us how many of these creatures stand above the throne of God. Most people think of them as being three in number. The three times that they cry "holy" might indicate to some that three is their number. But this is not positive, of course. Isaiah does reveal that they stand above the throne; therefore they have a ministry directly related to the throne of God. However, their ministry differs from that of the cherubim who stand beside the throne, for the seraphims have a ministry of heavenly chanting, or singing. It is their ministry to chant the praise of the character of God in heaven. They were no doubt beautiful creatures to look upon. The striking thing about them was their six wings. With two wings they covered their heads, a symbol of heavenly submission to their Creator. Two wings covered their feet as symbol of unfailing service to their Creator's commands. Two wings were used to fly. While it is commonly accepted that angels have wings to fly, which is not supported by the Scripture, yet the Bible does say that this special order of created beings used two of their wings to fly.

The glory of the seraphims is in their voices. They must possess beautiful musical voices to chant the praises of God for all of the heavenly host. Created by an infinite God, their harmonies must be perfect. Isaiah said their song was "Holy, holy, holy, is the Lord of hosts: the whole earth is full of his glory." When we consider the numberless host of angels, that is truly why God is called "the Lord of host." You will notice all through the Scriptures that when reference is made that God is the "Lord of host" it is generally related to the heavenly order of created beings.

How many angels make up this vast host of God we do not know. So many people limit their thinking to the existence of spiritual beings only to God and man. To some people man is the only spiritual being. To them the wide universe of worlds is a solitary place without inhabitants. It would seem incredible that man would be the only creature upon which God would lavish His love and blessing. Truly God has interests in other creatures besides man. If the only glory and honor God would receive would be from this solitary "star" it would not be much.

Satan, a Fallen Prince

Our Lord Jesus Christ called Satan "the prince of this world." Surely no such title would be given by Jesus Christ if it were not true. It is commonly accepted that we believe that Jesus died on the cross to pay a redemptive price not only for sinful men but also for the earth.

Under the Old Testament law, when a man redeemed a piece of land, he announced at the gates of the city that he was going to redeem a piece of land. After this announcement he took the elders of the city, as witnesses, to the piece of property. Standing upon the land, he would pay the price (the redemptive price) for it in the presence of the elders. They were witnesses to the redeeming. How beautifully this fits into the statement of Job: "I know that my redeemer liveth, and in the latter day he shall stand upon the earth." By faith

Job saw the Lord Jesus Christ as the "heavenly daysman," the Redeemer, standing upon the earth and paying the full redemptive price for it, to claim it for Himself.

In God's time, Christ is going to take Satan (the present prince) out of this world order (Rev. 20:1-3), and He is going to establish a new principality. It will be a kingdom of righteousness and holiness. Paul tells us in Romans chapter eight that the whole creation is groaning and waiting for this day of Christ's victory. This principality will be taken over by Jesus Christ and His heirs. The Church is described as that wonderful body that shall be the joint-heirs with Christ. This is a part of the rich reward that awaits the faithful in Jesus Christ. The prophets spoke of the wonderful day when the curse would be lifted. The lion and the lamb would again lie together. The nations would learn war no more.

Our Present-Day Hope

Romans 8:38 declares, "Neither death, nor life, nor angels, nor principalities...shall be able to separate us from the love of God...." The apostle Paul faithfully warned the Church that wicked, satanic forces war against it. But he also gave divine assurance to all believers that no angel (wicked) or principality of Satan has sufficient power to separate us from the love of Christ. We are, as the body of Christ, kept safe and secure in Him. The day of final triumph will come in God's good time.

Scientific progress and inventions make headlines. Wars make red the harvest fields of men with human blood. Human lives are filled and baffled by troubles and temptations. But Christ is building His Church. The song of victory—eternal victory—will be sung some day. Prepare yourself to stand with Christ and all His heavenly host on that day.

A Word on Tradition

Tradition has played an important place in human

history relative to angels. Before we leave this chapter of heaven's militant host, we should state our position on this matter.

A writer of exceptional ability and research, Huet, informs us that the belief of angels is found in the history of all nations. The ancient Egyptians, Phoenicians, Greeks, and others all expressed their belief in angels.

The Mohammedians believe in angels. They believe that two angels are assigned to each person. The angel on the right hand records all your good deeds. The angel on your left records all your evil deeds.

The Hebrews taught there were four great angels: (1) Gabriel, who reveals the secrets of God to men. (2) Michael, who fights and avenges God's foes. (3) Raphael, who receives the departing spirits of the dead. (4) Uriel, who will summon everybody to judgment.

Dionysius the Areopagite taught there were seven great angels, who are: Gabriel, Michael, Abdiel, Rognel, Raphael, Samiel, and Uriel.

Rabbinical Theosophy taught in later Hebrew history that there were seven great angels with the following names; Michael, Gabriel, Uriel, Chanruel, Jophiel, and Zodkiel and Raphael.

Please note that out of this list, presented in various traditions, only two are named in Scripture—Gabriel and Michael.

Angels in Literature and Art

Such writers as Dante and Milton devote large portions of their writings to descriptions of both good and evil angels. Many writers in ancient history give their descriptions of angels.

Michelangelo noticed a rough, rugged rock and said to his friends, "In that rough black rock my friends, I see an angel, and I mean to set him free." He followed a traditional concept of angels in his art. Michelangelo could paint pleasing pictures of angels as no other artist in history has been able to do. He painted them almost shadowless. He clothed them with the richest robes. Their heads were surrounded by golden nimbi. Their radiant wings were enameled in all the colors of the rainbow.

Whatever appreciation we may have of tradition as it is presented in religious teaching, literature, or art, we must remember to always take the Bible as the final authority. Dante and Milton give us excellent literature, but Jesus Christ and Paul give us our theology. We may read traditions with a degree of human interest, but it is Scripture upon which we base our faith for salvation.

8

Angels Meet Us at Calvary

Do angels assist us in our salvation? Our answer to this question is—yes! Many people hold the view that angels ministered to men before the Holy Spirit came in His fullness at Pentecost, but since that time this particular function of the celestial beings has ceased. But we cannot accept this conclusion. We contend that angels actually have a part in our salvation today and that they carry out "assisting ministries" to help the earthly pilgrim on his journey to heaven.

We thoroughly understand that it is the work of Jesus Christ on Calvary that atones for sin: He has redeemed us to Himself by His own broken body and shed blood. May nothing ever dim this blessed truth nor detract from the glorious work of our Savior on the cross! We also affirm that it is through the ministry of the gospel and the convicting power of the Holy Spirit that all sinners are "convicted" of their sins. Men are "born again" by the power of the Holy Spirit. But God uses both men and angels as instruments to bring the kingdom of God near to men.

Angels Minister to the Heirs of Salvation

The Scripture declares that angels are sent forth to minister to the people who have salvation. "Are they [angels] not all ministering spirits, sent forth to minister for them who shall be heirs of salvation" (Heb. 1:14)?

In the Book of Acts we see the work and power of the Holy Spirit, but who can read the glowing story of the conversion of Cornelius, as we find it recorded in the tenth chapter of Acts, without recognizing the reality of angels? In verse 30, Cornelius states that an angel stood before him in bright clothing and told him two thing.

First, the angel assured him that his relationship was right with God (verse 4). His prayers and alms were before God and known by the holy angels in heaven.

Second, the angel informed him what he should do to receive the baptism of the Holy Spirit. The angel commanded him to send for Peter and, furthermore, told him where Peter was—the city is named, as well as the man's name in whose home Peter was being entertained and the location of the house. This was the ministry of an angel.

Philip, recently elected deacon of the church at Jerusalem, was ordered by the angel to go down into the desert and preach.

> And the angel of the Lord spake unto Philip, saying, Arise, and go toward the south unto the way that goeth down from Jerusalem unto Gaza (Acts 8:26).

Philip obeyed the angel's orders. Soon he was standing in a chariot presenting Christ to a hungry heart! A remarkable conversion took place. Who can doubt the ministry of the angels? Peter's wonderful deliverance from prison was the work and ministry of an angel. The angel of the Lord appeared to John on Patmos and gave him the Book of Revelation.

Angels play a threefold part in our salvation:

First: Angels witness our salvation. These are the words of Jesus:

> Likewise, I say unto you, there is joy in the presence of the angels of God over one sinner that repenteth (Luke 15:10).

Angels do not rejoice when people reform or decide to live better in their own strength. But angels rejoice in heaven when sinners repent! You might fool your family, your neighbors, or even your church, but you cannot fool the angels. If you repent and find Jesus Christ as your Savior, all the angels in heaven know about it. Jesus said so.

Let the sinner confess his sin. Let him confess that Jesus died upon Calvary for him. Let him believe in Jesus Christ as his Savior—and there will be joy in the presence of the angels of God! This is still as true today as it was 1900 years ago when Jesus uttered these words. A person might find salvation alone, when separated from friends here on earth. It might truly be in the "secret place!" But rest assured that if he has done business with God in repentance all the angels know about it.

Second: Christ personally reports our confession or denial of Him before all the angels. One has well said, "The angels are our neighbors." Jesus Christ gives us some valuable information about heaven in this passage:

> ... Whosoever shall confess me before men, him shall the Son of man also confess before the angels of God: But he that denieth me before men shall be denied before the angels of God (Luke 12:8, 9).

He informs us that our confession of Christ on earth before men is reviewed in heaven's court! The recognition that we have among the royal angels is determined by our confession here on earth. What a glorious honor to have Jesus call our names as ones of His own before all the holy angels! What awe grips us as the Master declares that if we deny Him here on earth, the same denial will be announced by Jesus Christ in heaven's court! How it behooves us to honor Him while we are on earth.

The day you made your confession of Jesus Christ as your Savior, your name, yes, your name, was announced in heaven's court. Your name was recorded in the Lamb's Book of Life.

Third: The Lamb's Book of Life and the angels. We have often heard the remark, "the recording angel." I question if any angel is the keeper of the Book of Life. The Scriptures convey the thought that Jesus Christ Himself keeps the records in this book.

> ...I will not blot out his name out of the book of life; but I will confess his name before my Father and before his holy angels (Rev. 3:5).

This passage of Scripture reveals the fact that there is a "Book of Life."

Ancient cities kept a record book in which the names of all its citizens were recorded. A person could go to the city gate keeper and find if an individual was a citizen of that city. A name was never blotted out unless the individual lost his citizenship. The Scriptures tell us that the Christian is a citizen of heaven. Our names are recorded in the record book. In heaven this book is called "the Lamb's Book of Life." Wondrous Book! Only those who find salvation from sin through the blood of the Lamb of God are recorded in the Lamb's Book of Life.

Christ says of every citizen, that He will proclaim his name before His Father and all His angels. To proclaim your name before the Father is to declare your justified relationship with God. To proclaim your name before the angels is to announce your heavenly citizenship. Although you are a pilgrim and stranger on earth, you can look for a city to come whose builder and maker is God.

Blotted Out of the Book

There is one provocation that will cause Jesus to remove your name. John says that if we remove any part from the Book of Revelation—Jesus Christ will blot our names out of the Book of Life! You cannot keep your name in the Book of heaven if you trifle with the Book (Bible) down here. Believe and walk in the light of God's Word down here—and your name is safe forever in the Book of heaven!

The Lord has done all that is necessary to get each believer into heaven. Let us put our faith and confidence in our heavenly Lord and Savior, Jesus Christ. His angels are our ministering spirits.

9

Angelic Bodyguards for the Saints

Angelic visitations are never commonplace. Seldom in the history of God's people have their visitations been visible. One very important thing to consider in the history of their ministry to the saints in time of trouble is that their assistance is given to individuals when they have had a *divine service* to perform, but it was never done for personal benefit.

Peter's Bodyguard

And...the angel of the Lord came upon him, and a light shined in the prison; and he smote Peter on the side, and raised him up, saying, Arise up quickly. And his chains fell off from his hands. And the angel said unto him, Gird thyself, and bind on thy sandals. And so he did. And he saith unto him, Cast thy garments about thee, and follow me (Acts 12:7-9).

This angel awakened Peter, took the chains off his hands, gave him a light in which to dress, opened the doors of the Roman jail, and led him forth into the street. What a marvelous deliverance!

Peter's ministry was not yet finished. The angel of the Lord delivered him in a remarkable way. We must remember, however, not to glory in deliverance. Riches often come out of suffering. Many rich portions of both the Old and New Testaments came out of experiences of imprisonment. Nearly all of the writings of Paul came out of prison life. They can truly be called "the prison epistles." John wrote the Book of Revelation while he was a prisoner on the Island of Patmos. John Bunyan spent twelve years in Bedford jail, but *Pilgrim's Progress* came forth to bless weary pilgrims of generations to come.

Paul's Bodyguards

The angel of the Lord comforted Paul in a dreadful storm at sea.

> For there stood by me this night the angel of God, whose I am, and whom I serve, Saying, Fear not, Paul; thou must be brought before Caesar: and lo, God hath given thee all them that sail with thee (Acts 27:23, 24).

This angel from heaven assured Paul that all on board the ship would be preserved. No one can doubt after reading the story that it was the angel of God who saved Paul that night. You will notice also that this angel of God knew Paul's future—that he was destined to stand before Caesar and give his defense of the gospel in Rome. God was going to plant saints in Caesar's household! Paul had tried to warn the captain not to sail to Rome at this season, but he would not listen. Hardheaded captains may refuse counsel, and storms and wind may tear the boat to pieces, but God's man gets to Rome! Angelic bodyguards assisted Paul on his way.

Daniel's Bodyguard

The angel of the Lord clamped the mouths of the wild jungle beasts, and Daniel was spared. Daniel says the angel of God did it. "My God hath sent his angel, and hath shut the lions' mouths, that they have not hurt me" (Dan. 6:22).

We are not advised whether or not Daniel saw the angel or the angel talked with him. Both are possible. Whatever occurred that night, Daniel knew the secret of his safety. The angelic guard had been with him.

Angelic Firemen

A huge, black cloud of smoke drifted over the plains of Dura. Awesome flames were licking skyward as the servants of King Nebuchadnezzar placed more fuel on the fire. Three noble servants of God had refused to bow to the golden image of the king. Nebuchadnezzar chided them for their disobedience to the royal decree and mocked the idea of a God that could deliver three defenseless men from his wrath. He ordered the firemen to make the furnace seven times hotter than any fire that had ever burned before in Babylon. Men had never seen such a fire. When the men took the three Hebrew noblemen to throw them in, the angry, uncontrollable flames reached out and burned them to death. God "hath sent his angel, and delivered his servants that trusted in him" (Dan. 3:28).

Angelic firemen took charge of this roaring inferno and brought forth three of God's saints without the smell of fire upon their garments. One of the great wonders of glory, which will amaze every redeemed soul, will be the unfolding of God's love and care for him. Jesus prayed that His followers would get through to glory; and truly He manifests His matchless care to all His saints!

Angelic Ministry Among the Nations

The limited space in this book forbids us to call detailed attention to the important work of angels in the story of nations. From the time when the destroying angel went through the land of Egypt and delivered Israel from slavery, the stories of angelic deliverance have been many.

We have cited the guardian ministry of the angels to individuals and nations and to all who fear God. Many timid and fearful souls who read these pages can right now take great courage and faith. Why do you not this moment believe the Word of God? God is no respecter of persons. God has no favorites nor pets in His family. Believe in the care and love of your heavenly Father. The Scriptures inform us: "Are they [angels] not all ministering spirits, sent forth to minister for them who shall be heirs of salvation?" (Heb. 1:14).

The ministry of angels is not ancient history alone.

The apostle declares that angels minister to the heirs of salvation. If we could but realize this blessed truth, how much worry and fretting could be instantly cured! What calm assurance every child of God could have amidst life's storms and struggles! We as individual believers must mix the Word with faith as we read it, to receive its fullest benefits. No longer let your life be plagued with fear and distrust. Resolve now—deeply within yourself—to be a true child of faith and trust. Repeat—"I can, I will, I do believe!"

10

Sevenfold Protection of Jesus

There are seven crises in the life of Jesus Christ. In each of them we see the special ministry of angels.

The Pristine Glory and the Angels

Angels were with Christ when He created this world. "When the morning stars sang together, and all the sons of God shouted for joy" (Job 38:7). What beautiful harmony must have sounded forth in this angelic song! What shouts must have echoed through God's royal courts! If the angels played such an important part in the creation of this earth, why should we doubt the important part they play in all matters concerning this earth?

The Incarnation and the Angels

The angel of the Lord announced to Joseph and Mary the coming of Immanuel to this earth (Matt. 1:20-21).

The angel of the Lord told the humble shepherds that Jesus was born (Luke 2:8-15). He was the Lamb of God—therefore the announcement was given first to the shepherds. He, the Lamb of the ages, was born in a stable, the place where we think of lambs being born. Who could better understand the blessed story of the Lamb of God than these experienced shepherds of the hills?

Angels Worshiped Christ in the Stable

We have the record of the shepherds coming to the humble stable to give their honor to the Christchild. We have the account of the wise men coming later and worshiping the Child and giving their rich gifts to Him. We also have the story of angels worshiping at the manger crib! It was a great hour when the angels who had done His bidding in the heavenly courts before His incarnation came down and bowed in homage at the manger crib! No man was allowed to see this vision or behold its glory, but the Holy Spirit records this scene of angelic worship: " And again, when He bringeth in the first begotten into the world, he saith, And let all the angels of God worship Him" (Heb. 1:6).

A colt upon which no man had ever sat bore Him gently into Jerusalem while envy and murder rankled in the hearts of men who should have welcomed Him. A city that should have crowned Him led Him out and crucified Him! Angels worshiped and ministered to Him while men gave Him vinegar mixed with gall to drink. Angels shouted His praises while mobs of sinners cried, "Crucify Him!" Angels sought the glory of watching His every footstep, while sinners gloried in driving nails into His feet. Holy angels stood in awe, while men spit into His face. Angels called Him the Holy One, while men called Him a wine-bidder. What a fearful contrast. Angels worshiped while men crucified! With which group are you standing?

Angelic Ministry in Temptation

The Greek word for "minister" is *diakoneo* which means "to act as a deacon, to serve." With no earthly friends to assist Him, the angels came down to act as heavenly deacons. "Behold, angels came and ministered unto him" (Matt. 4:11). They gave Him the needed supply of comfort and strength for that hour.

Angels in the Garden

The Greek word for "strengthening" is *enesaiu,* which means to "make strong inwardly." This same word is used in Acts 9:19 when Paul who was nearly fainting received food and was strengthened. In the receiving of food, Paul's body was changed from weakness to strength. "And there appeared an angel unto him from heaven strengthening him" (Luke 22:43).

Jesus soon was to drink the bitter cup of anguish that climaxed on the cross. He needed this inward strength from heaven. The ancients had a custom that when a guest came he was assigned a cup. The host would fill this cup with wine. There were various qualities of wine made and served to guests in the home. If it was an ordinary guest or occasion, the poorest quality of wine was served. If an outstanding guest was present, the very best wine was served. Anyone could tell the honor accorded him by the host in the quality of wine served.

Jesus as servant was not honored with the best wine. He had to drink the bitter cup. The very dregs of God's displeasure against sin were in this cup. Holy angels came down and strengthened Jesus to drink the cup. Who would deny our Savior this precious ministry of the angels in this fearful hour?

Angels—The Royal Bodyguard

Angels were at the crucifixion:

> Thinkest thou that I cannot now pray to my Father, and he shall presently give me more than twelve legions of angels (Matt. 26:53)?

Pilate, the Roman governor, was informed by this humble, friendless prisoner that if He would ask His Father, His Father would dispatch more than twelve legions of angels. Jesus was speaking to a Roman governor. He knew a Roman legion was six thousand foot soldiers. Twelve times six thousand would make a royal bodyguard of 72,000.

Jesus knew how many angels were at His call that very moment. This royal bodyguard of 72,000 angels were ready to defend Him. But as the royal bodyguard drew near, the Savior waved them aside. The Scriptures say that Jesus laid down His life. In the light of such an astounding act of our Lord, who can doubt it? What must these royal bodyguards have thought when they saw their Lord fall beneath His cross? Any one of these angels would have counted it his endless glory to have lifted the beam from the weary shoulder!

The Three Royal Witnesses of the Resurrection

Three angels witnessed the resurrection. The first angelic witness is described by Matthew:

> And, behold, there was a great earthquake: for the angel of the Lord descended from heaven, and came and rolled back the stone from the door, and sat upon it. His countenance was like lightning, and his raiment white as snow: And for fear of him the keepers did shake, and became as dead men (Matt. 28:2-4).

This royal witness did not roll the stone away so Jesus could get out of the grave, but that earthly witnesses might look in and see where the Lord had lain.

This angel is described very briefly. His countenance was so dazzling that it appeared as lightning and struck the onlooking Roman soldiers with such fear that they became paralyzed, like dead men. His raiment was white as snow, which indicates that angels do wear a certain type of clothing.

Two other angelic witnesses are described by John:

> But Mary...looked into the sepulchre, and seeth two angels in white sitting, the one at the head, and the other at the feet, where the body of Jesus had lain (John 20:11, 12).

In the mouth of two or three witnesses shall every word be confirmed. Two angels sitting on the rock tomb told Mary, the weeping mother, that her son no longer was in the grave and to weep no more. One angel sitting on the outside on the rock used for the door to the tomb told the followers of Jesus not to look for the living among the dead—"He is not here—He is risen!"

In the earthly life of our Lord and Savior, the angelic ministry played a most important part. From the stable manger to the glorious resurrection, the angels never forsook their Creator and Master.

57

11

Guardian Angels in Childhood

A picture that deeply impressed me in childhood was an artist's conception of the guardian angels of children. A child was walking along a narrow path, dangerously close to the edge of a steep precipice. At his side was a beautiful angel with wings outstretched to protect him from falling. This vivid scene of protection and care made an impression upon my boyhood consciousness which never shall be forgotten.

Some people have ridiculed the idea of guardian angels; others have deviated so far from the Scriptures that their views border on the preposterous.

Children Do Have Guardian Angels

Jesus said,

> Take heed that ye despise not one of these little ones; for I say unto you, That in heaven their angels do always behold the face of my Father which is in heaven (Matt. 18:10).

This is rightly called the "Children's Chapter of the Bible." A child is mentioned seven times (note vss. 2, 3, 4, 5, 6, 10, 14). The disciples were arguing about who would be the greatest in the kingdom. Jesus took a child and taught the disciples a very pointed object lesson. He informed the disciples that small children are recognized in heaven. If the heavenly Father notes the fall of the sparrow, surély He beholds children.

Jesus said, "In heaven their angels do always behold the face of. my Father." According to Jesus, children do have guardian angels who stand in heaven with an unclouded vision of the heavenly Father. We shall see in a later chapter that these guardian angels have a ministry of representation in heaven, and many times an active and personal ministry on earth for God's children. I believe in guardian angels because Jesus Christ taught it. I believe in guardian angels because so many stories in both the Old and New Testaments prove it.

The psalmist said: "The angel of the Lord encampeth around about them that fear him, and delivereth them" (Ps. 34:7). This is a special promise to the trusting child of God. This promise alone has nerved the right arm of many a soldier of the Lord in His holy warfare. It has strengthened his faith in the darkest hour. It has fired his soul with courage in hours of apparent defeat.

It is very evident that Satan believes in guardian angels. This is clear in Matthew 4:6:

> And he saith unto him, If thou be the Son of God, cast thyself down: for it is written, He shall give his angels charge concerning thee: and in their hands they shall bear thee up, lest at any time thou dash thy foot against a stone.

Satan said, "It is written." Even he believes God's Word.

However, we do have here a vital lesson. Satan was tempting Christ to perform a reckless, unreasonable act—to defy all the natural laws of God's world. No man can break unwritten laws of nature and do right, any more than he can break the written law of God's Word and do right. To break the laws of nature and expect to compel God to rescue one is presumption, not faith. The man who places himself in unnecessary danger defies the natural laws of God's world and cannot expect divine deliverance.

Faith and obedience are inseparable. It is only in the line of duty that you can expect help from God. Do the will of the Father and then you can trust the heavenly Father no matter what dangers beset you.

12

Angels Bring Us Answers to Prayer

Do the angels bring answers to prayer? In what way does this phase of their ministry affect the Christian believer? In the consideration of this important subject we must always hold the correct perspective concerning our salvation and the work of the Holy Spirit. Angels do not save us from our sins; they do not minister grace to our hearts; they do not guide and inspire the believer in the study of God's Word. All the benefits of redemption in relation to Christian experience are made real to us through the Holy Spirit. It is the ministry of the Spirit to make Christ known to the hearts of men.

It is not the purpose of this book to direct attention unduly to angels nor in any way to diminish the glory of our Savior. The angels are "ministers" of God. Their ministry should not detract from Christ's glory. As the calling of the leaders of the Church is to exalt Christ, so the ministry of angels serves to exalt Jesus Christ.

After carefully searching the Scriptures we find that angels do have a place and part in the prayers of God's people. When prayer is a matter of communion, thanksgiving, and fellowship with our heavenly Father, angels have no part in it. "Go into thy closet and shut the door—and thy Father which seeth in secret...." Everyone and everything is shut out—except your heavenly Father. Anything less, is to come short in prayer.

The place of angels in prayer, however, seems to center about two things. First, when God has some prophetic vision or message for His servants, He often has directed angels from heaven to their assistance with answers to their prayers and special directions for their guidance.

Second, we see angels in relation to prayer when the safety and future ministry of one of God's chosen vessels is at stake.

Ministering to Cornelius

In the tenth chapter of Acts, the story of Cornelius shows clearly the ministry of angels at times of prayer. Verse two states that Cornelius was a devout man and prayed to God always. In verse three we are told the angel of the Lord spoke to him. Verse twenty-two informs us that Cornelius had told his servants and friends about the angel's visitation. In verse thirty Cornelius tells Peter that the angel who stood before him as he prayed was dressed in "bright clothing."

The reader will recognize that this was no ordinary day of prayer for Cornelius. This was the hour at which God's great timetable was changing. Jerusalem's day was closing. The Holy Spirit now was opening the door for the world-wide evangelization of the nations. The apostle Peter realized this. Peter's "housetop" vision from the Lord was timed with this angelic visitation. Peter says in verse thirty-four: "I perceive that God is no respector of persons."

This angelic visit to Cornelius therefore, came not in just an ordinary time of communion with God. It came as divine providence was opening the door of salvation to gentile nations—all nations were to receive the gift of the Holy Spirit. This was, no doubt, the first and last angelic visitation to Cornelius.

Ministry to Daniel

In the ninth chapter of Daniel we are told of the royal visit to Daniel in Babylon. The question often is asked whether or not angels need wings to fly. Many people considering the wings of a bird think of an angel propelling himself in like fashion. There are wings on our airplanes, but they do not operate as the wings of a bird. In verse twenty-one, Gabriel was made to "fly swiftly" to answer Daniel's prayer. When one considers the realm where these heavenly messengers travel, it is not a matter of wings; angels have a power of flight unknown to mankind.

Jesus ascended to heaven from the Mount of Olives as His disciples beheld Him, and His ascension was not a matter of wings. When Jesus comes again, the Church will ascend to meet Him in the air, and wings will not be necessary. The "New Jerusalem" shall descend from heaven—and that, too, will not require wings.

The seraphims, one rank of the angelic host, however, do have wings. The Bible mentions them as having six wings. We have considered the seraphims in chapters one and eight.

Gabriel's royal visit was not a result of Daniel's communion with his God. He was sent to inform Daniel of the Seventy Weeks of momentous Jewish history, and especially to foretell when the Messiah would come and reign as the "Ancient of days" (Dan. 7:22).

Peter's Deliverance

Peter's deliverance from jail by the angel of the Lord as the church prayed shows again the place of angels in our prayers at times of special divine providence. Thus the Scriptures reveal that angels minister only in times of prayer when special directions are needed by God's servants. They do not provide any spiritual grace or blessing to a believing heart in communion with Christ.

Their mission is not "spiritual." No one should judge his standing with God on the grounds of "angelic visitations." It is the Holy Spirit who bears witness with our spirits that we are the children of God.

13

Do Angels Preach the Gospel?

Angels cannot preach or proclaim the good news of salvation. The reason is not that angels are incapable of being wonderful messengers, but there are some things that are "exclusive" to man in this Church age. The Holy Spirit is the builder of Christ's Church. The Holy Spirit regenerates the sinner and gives him eternal life; He reveals the things of Christ to the believer and baptizes him into the Body of Christ; He empowers and anoints the Church for service. In His comprehensive plan of redemption, God chooses to "call men to preach"; it is by "the foolishness of preaching" that men are saved (I Cor. 1:18).

Three Reasons Why Only Men Can Preach

1. Only men can speak to men's hearts. The "changing things" in the changing ages do not change men's hearts. Whether men have driven in an ancient Roman chariot or are driving in a twentieth-century auto, their hearts have remained the same. Whether men plow with a crude plow or with a modern tractor, it still remains necessary that the fallow ground be broken up before the seed is planted. Only men can speak to men's hearts, for they know what the human heart needs. Angels are strangers to this heartfelt requirement.

2. Only men can understand the need of a Savior. When William Booth, the founder of the Salvation Army, was talking to King Edward of Great Britain, he said: "Some men's ambition is art; some men's ambition is fame; some men's ambition is gold; my ambition is to save the souls of men!"

This resulted from his famous Sunday afternoon walk —the walk in the back streets of London where he first saw the poor and the neglected and realized their helplessness and despair. On his return from that memorable walk, William Booth said to his companion, "Wife, something has to be done for the poor of London!" He knew they needed help; he felt it. Out of that passion a mighty army of Christian workers was born. Angels never could have felt such a need of humanity for a Savior to lift them out of their sin and sorrow.

3. *Only men can speak with a passion.* Paul said, "I am ready to preach" (Rom. 1:15). Paul had a gospel of absoluteness, of certainties, and a message of finality. Paul did not talk in generalities. To him the gospel was the power of God. It was not an age for "clouds by day" or "pillars of fire by night." These visible sights had served and their day had passed; a new day had come. A new power was manifest from God; its channel was the gospel.

It was a cool, brisk morning in Washington, D.C. (April 15, 1865) when Mr. Stanton, Secretary of War, knelt beside a bed. Lying before him was the gaunt and haggard form of a great man. At seven o'clock, Mr. Stanton arose from his knees, lowered the shades of the windows, looked back again at the silent form on the bed, and said, "Now he belongs to the ages."

This is the shortest biography of Abraham Lincoln. It was a gracious tribute to a great president, but it is only relatively true. His life and power were largely confined to his own nation.

But Jesus truly belongs to the ages. You cannot draw a line across the map and put Jesus just on one side. His influence embraces the whole world. You cannot say, "One race is all He will save," for His cry rings out, "Look unto me, ye ends of the earth and be saved!"

Paul said, "I am ready." The Greek word for "ready" does not mean intellectual preparation; it means a violent raging or the short, rapid breath of a runner. Paul

64

was assuring the Romans that, for him, preaching the gospel in Rome would be no irksome task. He was in the possession of a violent passion. His spirit was ready to burst from within like the breath exhaled by a hard runner.

The Holy Scriptures Speak of the "Day of the Lord"

Paul's charge to Timothy (II Tim. 4:2) still applies today:

> Preach the word; be instant in season, out of season; reprove, rebuke, exhort with all longsuffering and doctrine.

But there is a day coming when man's preaching will be done; the Church will have been raptured; and all the preachers' voices will be silent. This "Day of the Lord" is defined by Daniel as the Seventieth Week, or a period of seven years. It is also called "the tribulation period" and "the time of Jacob's trouble." During this fearful day of trouble and judgment, a mighty angel will give this world God's last call.

> And I saw another angel fly in the midst of heaven, having the everlasting gospel to preach unto them that dwell on earth, and to every nation, and kindred, and tongue, and people, Saying with a loud voice, Fear God, and give glory to him; for the hour of his judgment is come: and worship him that made heaven, and earth, and the sea, and the fountains of waters (Rev. 14:6-7).

The Message for the Ages

This fourfold call of the angel is God's message, the all-inclusive claim of God for the ages.

1. The call to fear God. Every son of Adam's race must stand before Jesus Christ. There is only one of two ways to face Him. Christ is before us as a suffering Savior. If we believe in Him as the Lamb of God, we shall be saved from the wrath to come. If we do not believe, we shall face Him as the judge of all the earth (Heb. 10:28-31).

It is Savior or Judge! Well may we fear the God of all the earth!

2. *The call to give glory to God.* Glory to God in the highest! Angels and the redeemed people of Christ, the Church, will swell the chorus of God's praise. All through the Scriptures we are commanded to praise the Lord.

3. *The announcement of the hour of judgment.* Peter says, "the Day of the Lord will come!" According to the Scriptures, sin has or will reach three fearful crises: two are past; one is to come.

First is the crisis of corruption. After the fall of Adam and the expulsion from Eden, sin raced on very rapidly. During the time of Noah, it reached its climax in indescribable corruption. The heart and imagination of man was evil beyond correction. The instrument of judgment was water, and the consummation was death.

Second is the crisis of crucifixion. Human sin reached its most awesome crisis when the Son of God was crucified. The instrument was the "cursed tree"; the victim was the "sinless Son," and the consummation was death. Sin with its blighting power and a million woes for humanity finds its lone conqueror in the Man of the middle cross. Christ tasted death for every man!

Third is the crisis of human and satanic rebellion. Daniel and John, the men of end-time vision, saw a day when men and fallen angels would join in a final stand against the Lord's anointed. This crisis will take place in the Valley of Armageddon. The instrument of judgment will be the "sword of Christ's mouth!" The consummation will be death for earth's mighty men!

4. *The call to worship.* Weary pilgrims are promised a day when the kingdom will come! The King's will shall be done on earth as well as in heaven. The peerless captain of Galilee shall have all things under His feet. From the least to the greatest, all shall worship the King. His holy train shall fill the earth as well as the heavenly temple. O worship the King.

But silence follows the call: There is no record of the nations heeding this last summons of God. This is the first and last time an angel has any ministry of calling men to God. The Church will be at the marriage supper of the Lamb. Her faithful servants will have finished the Calvary call of the gospel. God's last and final call, therefore, will be issued by an angel.

14

Angels—The Heavenly Watchers

All heaven is watching the mighty drama of this Church age. Conclusive Scriptural evidence is found in Ephesians 3:10:

> To the intent that now unto the principalities and powers in heavenly places might be known by the church the manifold wisdom of God.

The words "that now" are age long, taking in this entire dispensation, the Church age, from Pentecost to the Rapture. "That now" informs us that God has set the drama of the ages. All heaven is called to witness the building of the Church, the Body of Jesus Christ.

That Principalities and Powers in Heavenly Places Might Know

Paul clearly reveals that God is giving the "angelic rulers" of His vast dominion a revelation of His wonderful wisdom. As the Lord works grace, love, redeeming power, and holiness into the life of redeemed, regenerated mankind, angels are receiving an "observation lesson" of God's wisdom. Angels never would have known the awfulness of human sin had they not witnessed the crucifixion of God's Son. They never would have known the power of truth and holiness if they had not witnessed this great lesson as Christ builds His Church.

We cannot imagine the emotions aroused in the angels as they observe the power of sin broken by Jesus Christ. As they witness the building of holy character in human lives, the manifold wisdom of God is revealed to them. It is the wonderful drama of the ages!

The Angelic Theater

We read in I Corinthians 4:9:

> For I think that God hath set forth us the apostles last, as it were appointed to death: for we were made a spectacle unto the world, and to angels and to men.

The word "spectacle" (Gr. *theatron*) refers to the old Roman theater, or colosseum, which seated 80,000 people. In this great theater, the gladiators fought to entertain the emperor and pleasure-living Romans. The wicked hearts of the Romans became so depraved that men fought savage beasts of all kinds, such as wild bulls or half-starved lions. Rome reached the depth of her depravity when human beings—the Christians—were brought in and subjected to all kinds of torture for entertainment. Paul says this world is like a great theater and the angels are looking down and watching. Angels are watching every day how you stand up for Jesus Christ. They observe how you fight for truth and right.

Angels Witnessed Christ's Ordination

Sinful men could not judge the Holy One. Men called Jesus "Beelzebub," the "prince of devils." They chided Him for being a winebibber. They decreed He had a devil. That's what men think of holiness.

But angels watched and witnessed His holy conduct. "God was manifest in the flesh, justified in the Spirit, seen of angels...received up into glory" (I Tim. 3:16). If in the minds of men the sinless One was condemned, He surely was vindicated by God's holy angels! The high priest rent His garments and Roman soldiers applied the scourge and the mob cried, "Away with Him." But God the Father sent angels down to roll the stone away from the door of the tomb. He was received into glory. The priests and judges are dead—but He lives forever and ever!

Angels Witnessed Timothy's Ordination

Paul challenged Timothy, "I charge thee before God, and the Lord Jesus Christ, and the elect angels, that thou observe these things..." (I Tim. 5:21). Paul said, "I charge thee before God—and the angels." This really is a re-charge. Paul stirred up this young minister to a more careful discharge of his ministerial duties. He informed Timothy that God and the elect angels were observing him in the performance of his duties.

This world is a great theater. Angels are beholding us. What a solemn warning to every one of us. How carefully we should walk, and how carefully we should talk, for the angels are near!

15

How Did Holy Angels Sin?

There are seven great mysteries mentioned in the Bible, and sin is one of them. A mystery is something that is unrevealed. We recognize that the infinite mind of God understands all things; but there are some mysteries in the Word of God that have not been or cannot be explained in the realm of man's comprehension. The essence of sin is self-will against the will of God. This definition of sin holds in relation to both man and angels.

Shocking News—Angels Have Sinned

Peter wrote, "For if God spared not the angels that sinned, but cast them down to hell..." (II Peter 2:4).

The apostle Peter warns the apostolic Church that a "certain group" of angels had sinned. It is generally accepted among Bible scholars that angels sinned in heaven before the human tragedy of Genesis occurred. Sin was known first in heaven.

Jude wrote:

And the angels which kept not their first estate, but left their own habitation, he hath reserved in ever-lasting chains under darkness unto the judgment of the great day (v. 6).

Jude reveals that some of the angels left their divinely appointed places of rulership and power. Hell is a place prepared for the devil and his angels according to the teaching of Jesus. It would seem that if the doom and punishment of both angels and men will be the same eternally, then their sin must be somewhat related; that both committed the sin of rebellion.

There are two passages of Scripture that seem to describe the fall of a heavenly creature such as Lucifer. We recognize that all Bible scholars do not agree on the interpretation. Read the following two portions of God's Word and form your own conclusion. The Scripture passages are Isaiah 14:12-14 and Ezekiel 28:15.

Isaiah wrote:

How art thou fallen from heaven, O Lucifer, son of the morning: how art thou cut down to the ground, which didst weaken the nations: For thou hast said in thine heart, I will ascend into heaven, I will exalt my throne above the stars of God: I will sit also upon the mount of the congregation, in the sides of the north: I will ascend above the heights of the clouds; I will be like the most High.

The prophet Ezekiel said,

Thou wast perfect in thy ways from the day that thou wast created, till iniquity was found in thee.

Here was a being described as "created." Such reference is not made to mankind in general. The Bible speaks of "Adam" being created, but not his posterity. If these two Scripture passages can be accepted as descriptive of the fall of Lucifer, we would suggest the following study.

The Five "I Wills" of Isaiah 14

1. *"I will ascend into heaven."* This is suggestive of Satan's desire to occupy heaven as a supreme creature. He would possess it to the exclusion of all other creatures—angels and even God Himself. He would be the center of power and glory.

2. *"I will exalt my throne above the stars of God."* Here Lucifer would exalt his throne above all the rest of creation. He was not satisfied with his created position. Surely this is the essence of all rebellion.

3. *"I will sit also upon the mount of the congregation."* In the second "I will" is the open spirit of rebellion. Now we see the direct purpose of this creature. It is the brazen and wicked intent to dethrone God.

4. *"I will ascend above the heights of the clouds."* In this "I will," we see a creature whose imagination runs wild, and he pictures himself in a superlative position above all other kingdoms and powers.

5. *"I will be like the most High."* This creature would demand worship! Satan tried to induce worship to himself in the wilderness temptation. He offered Jesus all the kingdoms of the world if He would worship him! In foreign countries where pagan religions and the idol worshipers of heathenism prevail, missionaries come face to face with Satan's power in this regard.

Eve—The Goddess of Eden

We can discern how the pattern of Eve's fall in Eden is similar to the preceding study. Eve was not tempted to be lewd, sensual, or carnal. Not one thing was suggested to her to produce degenerate womanhood. "Eat," says the tempter, "and your eyes will be opened, and you will be gods." This was a direct temptation to be the goddess of Eden. It was a temptation to go upward, not downward. Eve discovered that such ambition led to rebellion against God. Expulsion from Eden followed her sin.

Lucifer Has Some Fallen Angels

The exact number involved in his power is not revealed in Scripture. But reference is made to his angels: "The dragon...and his angels" (Rev. 12:7).

Angels Await Judgment Day

There are fallen angels that will be brought forth for judgment. They will be sentenced and punished —forever for their sin—"...reserved unto judgment" (II Peter 2:4).

Christ's Announcement

According to Jesus Christ, hell is a prepared place of punishment for Lucifer and all his fallen angels "...everlasting fire, prepared for the devil and his angels" (Matt. 25:41).

Fallen Angels and Fallen Men—Same Hell

Both angels and men have rebelled against God. Mankind has a Redeemer in Jesus Christ, who can save them "from the wrath to come," if they will accept Him as their Savior. Angels have no Redeemer—and sinners who reject the only Savior will go to hell.

The moral nature of both man and angels who rebel is out of harmony with God, now and eternally. The rebels must go to prison. The Bible name for that prison house is hell.

16

Angelic War Prophesied

Satan, a fallen angel, has made a long stand against God. Ever since his rebellion when that mysterious force from within his being emanated into hatred for God, sin has written a dark and tragic story upon the annals of time. Satan, by the use of this powerful weapon in every day and age and clime, has waged a relentless war against the Creator. The forces of good and the forces of evil have continuously opposed each other in this battle of the ages, this conflict against sin.

The Battle of the Ages—Sin

Sin is a mystery, but we know what it does. "Fools make a mock of sin," but its tragic reality plagues us. What is it that lights the violent torch of war in lands of peace; makes red the harvest fields of man with human blood; leaves the empty chair and vacant room; destroys the best of mankind; and leaves millions of broken hearts? It is sin!

Sin smiles to deceive, sings to lure to destruction, and kisses to betray best friends. Sin hurls reason from its throne and drives men like mad Gadarene swine down the hill of time into the Lake of Fire. Sin like a hoary old sexton stands at the end of the trail, digging graves for all who transgress God's laws.

When will there be an end to this battle of the ages—this war against God—engendered in the heart of Lucifer, instigated by the serpent in the Garden of Eden, relentlessly continued through the days of the Old and the New Testaments, even to the tempting of the Son of God in the wilderness? It cannot go on forever. Man in his own strength has been unable to overthrow Satan in any way. Governments cannot legislate him out. He returns to mock the idealist. Education has made man the wiser to wage war. Today our twentieth-century civilization trembles on the brink of atomic destruction.

Only one Book in the world tells how right will finally triumph, and that book is the Bible.

> And there was war in heaven: Michael and his angels fought against the dragon; and the dragon fought and his angels...and the great dragon was cast out (Rev. 12:7, 9).

Angelic war is prophesied. Even as in the beginning when war was waged in heaven by the angels, so in the latter days the angels again will join in combat. Satan and his angels will make their last stand. No armies in history will have ever met in such a stupendous conflict. The battle of the ages at last shall reach its culmination. Fearful will be the tides of battle!

Heavenly News Flash!

What a news flash when the heavens echo with the victorious shout of Michael and his angels! What a glorious day this will be for the forces of righteousness! Eternal triumph will be the reward for all who stand with God and His Christ. A fearful day of eternal defeat will begin for all who have sided with the kingdom of Satan. What a day! Then the "deceiver of nations" shall be bound and put in his long prison house. Let all heaven rejoice with Jesus Christ, the King eternal! The believer knows that one day he will be shouting with the eternal victors.

Satan Removed

Ever since the day when man fell in the Garden of Eden and the curse descended upon this terrestrial sphere, all of nature has groaned in a minor key. Although God in His great love and mercy left many wonderful and beautiful things for man, who, though fallen, was still the object of His protection and care—the effects of the curse have never been lifted. The honeybee has a sting, the fragrant rose hides a thorn, and the handsome beast of the forest bares his fangs.

But, some glad day, the curse will be lifted from this earth, and Christ will reign in righteousness and power. The deserts will blossom with a thousand flowers. The hoary rocks will all be lichened. Sorrows will be transformed into joy. Every sin will be wiped away, and virtue will reign supreme. In the same pasture you will find the lion and the lamb grazing. Christ will be among His people as a shepherd among his sheep. Nothing shall harm nor molest in all His holy kingdom. Everyone should pledge his allegiance to Jesus Christ today!

17

Hell's Militant Host

A study of heaven's militant host is thrilling to the
heart of the believer. We are amazed when divine revelation permits us to witness some of the powers of
darkness. The Bible permits its readers to follow a trail
of truth concerning the final conflict—the end of Satan's
bloody reign.

The Unfinished Sentence

Our Lord Jesus once stood in the small synogogue
at Nazareth, His hometown. The village scribe handed
the Master the scroll of Isaiah. Facing a small audience
of friends and neighbors, He turned to Isaiah 61:1-2
(note Luke 4:19) for the reading. Christ closed the reading in the middle of a sentence, in verse 2—"to proclaim
the acceptable year of the Lord." Stopping at that place,
Luke says, "He closed the book."

This is dramatic and very significant, for the next state-
ment reads, "and the day of the vengeance of our God."
To proclaim the acceptable year of the Lord was our
Master's mission. It is also the mission of His Church.
The voice of the Church has echoed these many
generations—"This is the day of salvation!"

But the day will come when Christ will open the Book
of Isaiah again and carry to completion that unfinished
sentence—"the day of vengeance." The work of a kinsman was not only to redeem lost property; he was also
the avenger. He had to see that anyone who killed his
loved ones was duly punished.

Christ—the Kinsman Avenger

The kinsman Redeemer is destined to meet Satan—the master murderer (John 8:44)—and his wicked plotters. According to the prophets, Satan will maneuver his numberless host in the Valley of Armageddon for two purposes: first, to exterminate the Jews from the face of the earth; second, to entrench his militant host to prevent Jesus Christ from returning to the earth in His second advent. Satan knew God's plan called for Jesus to be born in Bethlehem in His first advent. He knew the time and place of this first advent.

Jesus, the Shepherd King, Shall Win

Wonderful truth is many times revealed to us in the history of the past. The types and shadows reveal so much.

Israel was challenged by Goliath, the champion of the Philistines. No man dared to go out to fight him. But David, the shepherd boy, went forth and slew him with one stone!

When Satan marshals his military might in the Valley of Armageddon, what can withstand such an array of power? Here will be gathered the united forces of Satan and mankind—the captains and generals of all the nations of the earth with their equipment of war that makes the earth tremble at the sight. Here will be Satan's attempt for the climaxing scheme of the ages—the annihilation of the Jews and the prevention of Jesus' second advent on Mount Olivet.

Christ shall prevail. The power of His Word shall smite the numberless host. Flesh shall fall from bones, for men shall be consumed in His wrath. He shall tread the winepress of His wrath alone. Blood shall flow to the horses' bridles. This will be the day of days!

Hell's militant host shall go down to eternal ruin and defeat. But the angels and the redeemed Church shall be secure! The Shepherd King shall prevail. If the maidens shouted, "Saul has slain his thousands, but

David his tens of thousands," when Israel celebrated this victory over Goliath, I wonder what the angels and the redeemed Church will shout on this day? Blessed be our kinsman Redeemer! Glory and honor be to our champion King, the Lord of host! Let His praises roll through the ages!

18

Angelic "Policemen" on Earth

The greatest movement of the ages will be the return of the Lord Jesus Christ. The Scriptures foretell the wonderful news that all the holy angels of heaven are coming with Him. This comprises so vast a host that no man can comprehend its number.

Advance Notice of This Train

Jesus predicted: "For the Son of Man shall come in the glory of his Father with his angels" (Matt. 16:27).

Jesus announces two things about His royal train:

First: He is coming in the glory of His Father. This means He is coming with a full revelation of His deity. Humanity has never seen this glory. Moses did not see it on Sinai. The disciples did not witness it on the Mount of Transfiguration. This day Jesus will shine forth in all the glory of His deity, a glory we cannot describe.

Second: 72,000 angels will form the special bodyguard of Jesus Christ. He told Pilate that He could have twelve legions of angels. If we consider a Roman legion, this would be 72,000 angels. What a royal bodyguard! Presidents and kings usually have several, but only Jesus will have 72,000. Jesus Christ robed in all His glory will be accompanied by 72,000 angels in His royal train.

All Heaven's Host in Attendance

Jesus laid aside all His glory to come and redeem mankind. Jesus stated that He is coming in His own glory; that is, as the heir—the rightful One—to take up His Kingdom. He is going to sit on His own throne—that will be His glory. Jesus further said that all the angels of heaven are coming with Him.

> When the Son of Man shall come in his glory, and all the holy angels with Him, then shall he sit upon the throne of his glory (Matt. 25:31).

These verses of Scripture are the words of Jesus Himself. Who dares doubt such authority?

The Early Church Preached This Fact

The Lord Jesus shall be revealed (the Greek implies "unveiled"). The world shall see Him in all His glory. Paul states that Jesus will come with all His mighty angels, and that the angels will bring judgment on those that obey not the gospel.

> And to you who are troubled rest with us, when the Lord Jesus shall be revealed from heaven with his mighty angels, In flaming fire taking vengeance on them that know not God, and that obey not the gospel of our Lord Jesus Christ (II Thess. 1:7-8).

Advance "Photo" of His Coming

The Word of God gives a vivid picture of just how He is coming.

Christ will come as heaven's outstanding horseman:

> And I saw heaven opened, and behold a white horse; And he that sat upon him was called Faithful and True, and in righteousness he doth judge and make war.
>
> His eyes were as a flame of fire, and on his head were many crowns; and he had a name written, that no man knew, but he himself.
>
> And he was clothed with a vesture dipped in blood: and his name is called The Word of God.
>
> And the armies which were in heaven followed him upon white horses, clothed in fine linen, white and clean (Rev. 19:11-14).

The horse is the only animal that is mentioned as being in heaven. Jesus will be riding a white horse! He had spent thirty-three years on earth and always walked. The prophets had spoken, and to fulfill Scripture, He one day rode into Jerusalem upon a colt, a colt upon which no man had ever sat (Matt. 21:4-11). This fulfilled the prophecy of Zechariah 9:9.

Jesus will come back to Jerusalem, riding upon a white horse. He is heaven's outstanding horseman. All the armies of heaven will follow Him, also riding on white horses.

The Special White Horse Cavalry Division

Jude tells us about a special white horse cavalry division. How many divisions there are in Christ's great host no man can number.

Enoch...the seventh from Adam, prophesied of these, saying, Behold, the Lord cometh with ten thousands of His saints to execute judgment... (Jude 14, 15).

There will be more than this number of saints in heaven. But Jude tells us that Enoch prophesied that a special battalion would lead Christ's hosts—a special white horse division 10,000 strong!

Angelic "Policemen" on Earth

Angelic "policemen" will assist Christ as He sets up His throne and kingdom to reign on David's throne for one thousand years. This will be no small task when you consider the machinery necessary for one ruler to take the reins of this entire world.

So shall it be at the end of the world: the angels shall come forth, and sever the wicked from among the just (Matt. 13:49).

We have here angels separating the wicked from the just. In another place it is described as the separation of the goats from the sheep.

There will be no escape from God's angelic "policemen."

The harvest is the end of the world; and the reapers are the angels (Matt. 13:39).
And shall cast them into the furnace of fire: there shall be wailing and gnashing of teeth (Matt. 13:50).

Jesus has sent forth the sowers with the good seed. The enemy has sown tares. But the angels are the reapers at the end of the age.

The Son of man shall send forth his angels, and they shall gather out of his kingdom all things that offend, and them which do iniquity; And shall cast them into a furnace of fire...(Matt. 13:41-42).

19

Angels at the River

Jesus told a parable about "a certain rich man" and "a certain beggar named Lazarus."

> ...The beggar died, and was carried by the angels into Abraham's bosom: the rich man also died, and was buried (Luke 16:22).

Here we see a great contrast as far as the world goes: a very wealthy man accustomed to all the luxuries and honors of his station, and the lowest in the social scale—a poor beggar, full of sores, who begged for the crumbs that fell from the rich man's table.

They both died. It is stated that "the rich man was buried." Undoubtedly he had a pompous funeral—a long procession of mourners, a eulogy of his wonderful works and benevolences, and a stately monument erected over his grave. It is not even mentioned that the beggar was buried; probably he was just thrown into a hole somewhere and the dirt quickly shoveled over his body. But he was a believer in God, and his spirit belonged in the realms of the just. So he was carried by the angels—not just one, but an escort of angels—into Abraham's bosom, which the Jews called the paradise of the righteous.

Everyone is going to die; there is no escaping this fact. The one important factor is faith in Christ. He tasted death for every man by the grace of God. He has the victory over death. The Scriptures and the Holy Spirit give gracious, unfailing support to all God's children at death. However, every Christian should be interested in all the ministries of God at this hour. What words of encouragement—"angels carried him!" If we can trust anyone to tell us the truth it is Jesus Christ, and He tells us that this unknown, neglected, and outcast beggar, who believed in God, had a royal escort of angels to take him to glory.

I won't have to cross Jordon alone;
Jesus died for my sins to atone.
In the darkness I see;
He'll be waiting for me.
I won't have to cross Jordan alone.

It is well, by the grace of God, that we enjoy life. It is not God's plan that our lives should be mournful, because we shall all too soon come to the end of the trail of life. It shall be no tragedy to die. God's royal escorts will not fail us. It matters not if His children be beggars or kings. He knows all His sheep by name. The way of the cross leads home. We shall exchange our cross for a crown.

No costly monument may mark your resting place. Your name may never be recorded in history for great accomplishments on this earth. In Christ's kingdom those poor in worldly wealth and fame can be rich in faith. This comforting thought is strengthened by the promise of Jesus that not a sparrow falls without His Father's notice. If a sparrow has value, of how much more importance is the value of His saints.

Beyond the Angels

We may be carried to Abraham's bosom by angels —but what's beyond? Abraham's resting place is not our eternal goal. The resurrection of Jesus was more than a resuscitation of a dead body. When Jesus arose from Joseph's tomb, He had a transformed body. His entire body—His whole personality—was on a higher plane. Christ's resurrection was truly a release. It was more—it was a glorious emancipation for Him. The apostle Paul informs us that Christ's resurrection is a pattern of what the Church will have through Him. His destiny is our destiny. In Him redeemed humanity will be glorified.

Jesus, King of Angels and Men

Jesus Christ is the divine cohesion of the universe. Some scientists say that the stability of the earth is determined by the law of gravity; but the law of gravitation is His law. Gravity may give stability to the earth, but Christ "upholdeth all things" by the word of His power.

The day is coming when the curse of Adam's sin will be lifted. The humiliated King, who was crucified, whose crown was thorns and whose scepter was a broken reed, is destined to reign over angels and men. Angels and redeemed men will crown Jesus Christ with many crowns. He shall reign over all the earth in holiness, righteousness, justice, and peace. As the forerunner within the veil, He has entered before us, to prepare the way and to receive His people. A heavenly train of the redeemed shall follow Him when He returns. The haven of rest is at the end of the voyage!

20

Worship of Angels Forbidden

The highest expression of honor and adoration the creature can give its Creator is worship. The unquestionable evidence of human depravity is perverted worship. Idolatry is the highest insult to God. God is a jealous God. His eternal command is: "Thou shalt have no other gods before me" (Exod. 34:14). The indisputable evidence of man's fallen nature and the depth of its spiritual darkness is not only revealed in the gross immoralities of the flesh, but also in the perverted worship of the spirit of mankind. The sins of sensuality may defile the flesh and demoralize society, but the depravity of man's spiritual nature is seen when he debases his spiritual nature in idolatrous worship.

Satan's vanity is witnessed in his determination to dethrone God and establish himself as the object of heavenly worship (note Isa. 14:14). For this vain ambition and blasphemous spirit he was cast out of heaven.

Satan Lures the Second Adam

Satan and the Second Adam, Jesus Christ, settled this issue in the wilderness temptation of Christ. Satan sought to lure Christ to "worship him" with the dazzling offer of the kingdoms of the world. It was a colossal award—all the kingdoms! But the price was awesome, too! Would the undefiled spirit of Jesus yield to this Satanic subtilty? No! The first Adam had failed in a beautiful garden, but the second Adam was victorious in a wilderness! The answer of Christ will be the pattern of the ages for heaven and earth—"Thou shalt worship the Lord thy God, and Him only shalt thou serve." Satan will never achieve his unholy ambition of being the object of universal adoration.

Satan's Fearful Title—Murderer

Satan is not a creature of life, but of death. Jesus ascribed to him the title of "murderer" (John 8:44). Satan is the one who destroys life; Jesus is the one who imparts life. Jesus draws men because He is life.

Satan's Subtle Plan

Satan was defeated by the Second Adam. The Church, the Body of Christ, has withstood his subtle purposes and maintained the pure spirit of worship on the earth. When the Church is raptured into the heavenlies, there will be no force to withstand Satan's plans.

Satan lured Adam and Eve by offering them something to eat, the forbidden fruit. He sought to weaken the defensive spirit of Jesus in the wilderness by enticing Him to make bread out of the nearby stones. Jesus proved to Satan that man can be victorious over physical appetite by the power of God.

A Shocking Scheme—666

According to Revelation 13, Satan will humble the nations with hunger. The world has rejected Jesus, the Bread from heaven, even as Israel rejected the manna.

> And he causeth all, both small and great, rich and poor, free and bond, to receive a mark in their right hand, or in their foreheads: And that no man might buy or sell, save he that had the mark, or the name of the beast, or the number of his name. Here is wisdom. Let him that hath understanding count the number of the beast: for it is the number of a man, and his number is six hundred threescore and six (Rev. 13:16-18).

In simple words, it is this, "If you want to eat—worship me!" (But, "what is a man profited if he shall gain the whole world, and lose his soul?") So Satan appears to win—but it is only for forty-two months (Rev. 13:5). Then follows his eternal loss—and what a loss!

Holy Worship

A few places in the Scripture permit us to see worship. We see a pure form of worship in the tabernacle and in the temple. Worship cannot be described as just one thing; it is rather a combination that blends so beautifully that it would be difficult to distinguish one part from another. The chief characteristics of worship are praise and adoration, oblation and sacrifice, prayer and communion.

In heavenly worship there is one thing which is outstandingly different from all earthly worship, and that is the attention given to God's written Word. In the Old Testament the law was read by the priest, the scribe, or the king. Jesus set the pattern in the New Testament by giving emphasis to the authority of the Scriptures. This has been followed in the New Testament by what we understand as the God-called and ordained minister. The souls of redeemed men live by the Word of God.

Angels, however, must never be the objects of worship. We may reverence them as wonderful servants of God ministering to man. John, as sincere as he was in his devotion to Christ, fell at the feet of the angel that talked to him on Patmos. But the angel forbade him to worship him. He commanded John to stand up and worship God alone (Rev. 19:10).

There is only one Being worthy of worship, and that is God. The Colossian church yielded to the temptation and started the worship of angels. Paul wrote them his timely epistle and chided them severely for this sin. "Let no man beguile you of your reward in a voluntary humility and worshipping of angels..." (Col. 2:18).

Angel worship, and all image worship, puffs up the flesh. Men glory in what they see, and they forget God. God is a jealous God. He will not share worship with any of the angelic host.

21

An Angel Stops the Clock of Time

A day is coming when the clock of time will stop. An angel will call a halt to the universe, and there will be an end to life as it is today. This great Day of the Lord—the fear of which is inherent in the heart of man —will begin a new era for every living creature. For centuries, man apart from his Creator has considered this day with great trepidation and dreadful forebodings. Even without gospel light, the heathen speak of a day when time shall be no more.

Since the earliest records of civilization, man has been interested in that mysterious, unfathomable something called "time," and has spent countless hours trying to measure it, recalling what has happened, and conjecturing what will come to pass in the future.

Man looked to the skies for his first help, observing that the sun made its journey through the sky at regular intervals. The moon and the stars also were considered when the discovery was made that they, too, ran according to a regular, accurate course. Then men learned to study the stars, and from them deducted great and wonderful facts.

They devised a way of measuring time based on the principle that the sun's course takes a year, and the moon passes through its different phases once every month, or thirty days. The days were named after the seven planets, which were symbolized as gods and goddesses, and each in turn was worshiped on a separate day—the sun, the moon, Jupiter, Mars, Venus, Saturn, and Mercury. This made the week, the month, the year. Various changes were made before the establishment of our present calendar, known as the Gregorian calendar, which was inaugurated in 1582.

The first crude time-telling device was no doubt a shadow falling at a certain time upon some stationary objects such as a rock or wall. From this developed the sundial with its various stages of improvement. The first mention of a sundial in the Bible is found in Isaiah 38.

Most people are familiar with the sandglass. They were often used when public speakers had a tendency to speak too long and too glibly. They even found their way in colonial America to the very pulpits of the worthy divines. One- or two-hour glasses were used to determine the stopping points of the sermons.

Through various ways and means, by genius, craftsmanship, and experimentation, the time-telling instruments have been perfected, resulting in the wonderful devices which we have today—all man's inventions to measure the passing of time and to foretell what is going to happen in the future.

This is the machine age, the age of invention, the age of man. So powerful has man become, so mighty the works of his hands, that he has forgotten God—the almighty Creator of all things—the Recorder of time and eternity!

Men have rebelled against God. They have broken His commandments, spurned His love, and heaped their insults upon His Son, the Lord Jesus Christ. They have made their own laws, formed their own moral codes, and built their own towers of Babel into the sky. There seems to be no end to the mechanical genius of man—but God has stopped things before. He stopped things at the Flood. He stopped things in Sodom and Gomorrah. He stopped things in Babylon in the night of Belshazzar's infamous banquet.

Christ spoke of a great coming judgment. The most forceful figures in language are used by Jesus Himself to describe this coming night. In Luke 21:34, it is spoken of as a "snare," something that shall come without general warning, as an overwhelming surprise. In Matthew 27:37, we read that it shall come while men are in the midst of a social whirl of courtship and marriage, physical gormandizing—living under a dark blanket of a spiritual blackout—"They knew not!"

The old world was too busy. They had left God out of their plans. The night shadows fell upon a world in Noah's time. Safety and hopes of tomorrow were found only by those within the ark.

The men of Sodom and Gomorrah were exceedingly sinful and refused to heed the warnings of God. Sudden destruction came upon them, with only Lot and his two daughters escaping.

The festive night in Babylon ended in tragedy. A thousand lords—attired in regal robes and wearing jewel-studded crowns of gold, lords of a mighty empire and heroes of battlefields—joined to celebrate triumph and glory. In the luxurious palace, banquet tables decorated with golden vessels were laden with choice foods of the kingdom. Wine flowed freely. A youthful king led the revelers in a night of sensual pleasure. But the night came. The voices of song and laughter suddenly died. An awesome hand wrote on the plaster of the wall, above the lampstand, at the king's table: *"Mene, mene, tekel, upharsin."* Faces turned ashy white, the terrified revelers shook with fear as the prophet Daniel interpreted: "God hath numbered thy kingdom, and finished it, ...Thou art weighed in the balances, and art found wanting, ...Thy kingdom is given to the Medes and the Persians."

Mankind today is standing with hands full of gold, but without God; playing with silver, but with no time for salvation; trusting that civilization will save them, but without Calvary. With laughter in their hearts at their shameful sins, they leave God out of their hearts. They are hurrying on their way while the harvest day slowly but surely passes. They continue counting their heaps of gold, but they win no souls. Basking in the summer sunshine, unmindful of the winter blast, they are dreaming of earthly security while neglecting the great salvation of Christ.

Those are fearful words—"He cometh!" There was a moment in history when awful darkness covered Egypt —but Israel had light! The world now is facing the day when the long shadows of the eternal night will push the last rays of the day away, when the cry of the ages will be heard—"Time shall be no more!"

> And the angel which I saw stand upon the sea and upon the earth lifted up his hand to heaven and sware by him that liveth for ever and ever, who created heaven, and the things that therein are, and the earth, and the things that therein are, and the sea, and the things which are therein, that there should be time no longer (Rev. 10:5, 6).

It is thrilling to see how this great angel proclaims Jesus to be what so many men have denied Him to be! He is declared to be the creator of three spheres —heaven, earth, and sea.

The angels sang their songs and shouted for joy as God created this world. The angels bore their flaming swords at Eden's gate; they administer judgment upon nations and people; they extend their guardian ministry to the saints; and angelic "policemen" will assist Jesus in His kingdom. Are you ready for the angel to cry, "Time shall be no more"? When the shores of the seven seas are dumb; when the waters lie pulseless forever; and the plains are cold; when the mountains fall from their majestic heights and all the islands move out of their places; when the sun wipes the death damp from the face of the earth for the last time; when the dying agonies of the universe begin; when the angel cries, "Time shall be no more—" will you be found in that day sheltered in the Rock of Ages?